THE COLLECTED WORKS OF
F. A. Hayek
VOLUME I

THE FATAL CONCEIT
The Errors of Socialism

PLAN OF THE COLLECTED WORKS
Edited by W. W. Bartley, III

The plan is provisional. Minor alterations may occur in titles of individual books, and several additional volumes may be added.

THE COLLECTED WORKS OF
F. A. Hayek

VOLUME I

THE FATAL CONCEIT
The Errors of Socialism

EDITED BY

W. W. BARTLEY III

The University of Chicago Press

The University of Chicago Press, Chicago 60637
Routledge, London

© 1988 by F. A. Hayek
All rights reserved. Originally published 1988
University of Chicago Press edition 1989
Printed in the United States of America

Library of Congress Cataloging-in-Publication Data

Hayek, Friedrich A. von (Friedrich August), 1899–
The collected works of F. A. Hayek.

Bibliography: v. 1, p.
Includes indexes.
Contents: v. 1. The fatal conceit.
1. Economics. 2. Free enterprise. 3. Liberalism.
4. Social sciences. I. Bartley, William Warren,
1934–   . II. Title.
HB171.H426   1989   330.1   88-26763
ISBN 0-226-32068-5 (v. 1)

∞ The paper used in this publication meets the minimum
requirements of the American National Standard for
Information Sciences—Permanence of Paper for Printed
Library Materials, ANSI Z39.48–1984

THE COLLECTED WORKS OF F. A. HAYEK

Published with the support of

The Hoover Institution on War, Revolution and Peace,
Stanford University
Cato Institute, Washington DC
The Centre for Independent Studies, Sydney
Earhart Foundation, Ann Arbor
Engenharia Comércio e Industria SA, Rio de Janeiro
Escuela Superior de Economia y Administración de Empresas
(ESEADE), Buenos Aires
The Heritage Foundation, Washington DC
The Institute for Humane Studies, George Mason University
Institute of Economic Affairs, London
Instituto Liberal, Rio de Janeiro
Charles G. Koch Charitable Foundation, Wichita
The Vera and Walter Morris Foundation, Little Rock
Swedish Free Enterprise Foundation, Stockholm
Timbro/Ratio Publishing House, Stockholm
The Wincott Foundation, London

CONTENTS

vii

CONTENTS

EDITORIAL FOREWORD

I

The Fatal Conceit, a new work by Hayek, is the first volume to appear in The Collected Works of F. A. Hayek, a new standard edition of his writings.

The reader who is struck by the pace and freshness of the argument of this new book, its vigorous application to specific cases, and its occasionally polemical thrust will want to know something of its background. In 1978, at the age of nearly eighty, and after a lifetime of doing battle with socialism in its many manifestations, Hayek wanted to have a showdown. He conceived of a grand formal debate, probably to be held in Paris, in which the leading theorists of socialism would face the leading intellectual advocates of the market order. They would address the question: 'Was Socialism a Mistake?'. The advocates of the market order would argue that socialism was – and always had been – thoroughly mistaken on scientific and factual, even logical grounds, and that its repeated failures, in the many different practical applications of socialist ideas that this century has witnessed, were, on the whole, the direct outcome of these scientific errors.

The idea of a grand formal debate had to be set aside for practical reasons. How, for instance, would the representatives of socialism be chosen? Would socialists themselves not refuse to agree on who might represent them? And even in the unlikely event that they did agree, could they be expected to acknowledge the real outcome of any such debate? Public confessions of error do not come easily.

Yet those of his colleagues who had met with Hayek to discuss the idea were reluctant to abandon it, and encouraged him to set down, in a manifesto, the main arguments in the free-market case. What was intended as a brief manifesto first grew into a large work in three parts; then the whole was compressed into the short book – or longer manifesto – presented here. Some fragments of the larger work have been preserved, and will be published separately in Volume X.

Adopting an economic and evolutionary approach throughout, Hayek examines the nature, origin, selection and development of the differing moralities of socialism and the market order; he recounts the extraordinary powers that 'the extended order' of the market, as he calls it, bestows on mankind, constituting and enabling the development of civilisation. Hayek also weighs – in a manner occasionally reminiscent of Freud's *Civilisation and Its Discontents*, yet reaching very different conclusions – both the benefits and costs of this civilisation, and also the consequences that would ensue from the destruction of the market order. He concludes: 'While facts alone can never determine what is right, ill-considered notions of what is reasonable, right and good may change the facts and the circumstances in which we live; they may destroy, perhaps forever, not only developed individuals and buildings and art and cities (which we have long known to be vulnerable to the destructive powers of moralities and ideologies of various sorts), but also traditions, institutions, and interrelations without which such creations could hardly have come into being or ever be recreated.'

II

The Collected Works of F. A. Hayek attempts to make virtually the entire Hayek corpus available to the reader for the first time. The chief organisation is thematic, but within this structure a chronological order is followed where possible.

The series opens with two closely-related books on the limits of reason and planning in the social sciences – *The Fatal Conceit*, a new work, and *The Uses and Abuses of Reason: The Counter-Revolution of Science, and Other Essays*, a work never previously published in Britain. The series continues with two collections of historical and biographical essays (*The Trend of Economic Thinking: From Bacon to Cannan* and *The Austrian School and the Fortunes of Liberalism*). The essays in these two volumes have never before been collected; over half of them have previously been available only in German; and approximately one-quarter of the first of these volumes is drawn from important manuscripts never previously published.

The series continues with four volumes encompassing the bulk of Hayek's contributions to economics: *Nations and Gold*; *Money and Nations*; *Investigations in Economics*; and *Monetary Theory and Industrial Fluctuations*.

These volumes are followed by three volumes of documentation, historical record and debate: *The Battle with Keynes and Cambridge*; *The Battle with Socialism*; and the remarkable *Correspondence Between Karl Popper and F. A. Hayek*, extending over fifty years, in which these close friends and intellectual collaborators intensely debate the main problems of philosophy and methodology, and many of the principal issues of our time.

These documentary volumes are followed by two new collections of essays by Hayek, and by a volume of his interviews and informal conversations about both theoretical issues and practical affairs – *Conversations with Hayek* – a volume intended to make his ideas available to a wider readership.

These first fourteen volumes will draw on, and be in large part created from, the resources of the large Hayek Archive at the Hoover Institution on War, Revolution and Peace, Stanford University, as well as its closely-related Machlup Archive and Popper Archive. Numerous other rich archival resources throughout the world will also be used. The first volume in the series, *The Fatal Conceit*, which is fresh from Hayek's hand, is of course unburdened by critical apparatus. The texts of subsequent volumes will be published in corrected, revised and annotated form, with introductions by distinguished scholars intended to place them in their historial and theoretical context.

The series will conclude with eight of Hayek's classic works – including *The Road to Serfdom, Individualism and Economic Order, The Constitution of Liberty*, and *Law, Legislation and Liberty* – books that are at the moment still readily available in other editions. It is assumed that the publication of the entire series will take ten to twelve years.

It is the intention of the editors that the series of volumes be complete in so far as that is reasonable and responsible. Thus essays which exist in slightly variant forms, or in several different languages, will be published always in English or in English translation, and only in their most complete and finished form unless some variation, or the timing thereof, is of theoretical or historical significance. Some items of ephemeral value, such as short newspaper articles and book notices of a few lines written when Hayek was editing *Economica*, will be omitted. And of course the correspondence to be published will be mainly that which bears significantly on Hayek's literary and theoretical work in economics, psychology, biography and history, political theory, and philosophy. All materials used in the creation of these volumes, as well as those comparatively few items omitted, will be available to scholars in the Hoover Institution Archives.

III

The preparation of a standard edition of this type is a large and also expensive undertaking. First and foremost among those who are to be thanked for their very great assistance are W. Glenn Campbell, Director of the Hoover Institution on War, Revolution and Peace, Stanford University, for the generous decision to provide the principal underlying support for this project, and also for the editor's biography of Hayek.

The presiding genius behind the larger project, without whose advice and support it never could have been organised or launched, is Walter S. Morris, of the Vera and Walter Morris Foundation. Two other institutions whose directors watched carefully over the inception of the project, and whose advice has been invaluable, are the Institute for Humane Studies, George Mason University, and the Institute of Economic Affairs, in London. The editor is particularly indebted to Leonard P. Liggio, Walter Grinder, and John Blundell, of the Institute for Humane Studies; and to Lord Harris of High Cross and John B. Wood, of the Institute of Economic Affairs. Equally important has been the unflagging support and advice of Norman Franklin of Routledge & Kegan Paul, Ltd., London, who has been Hayek's publisher for many years. Finally, the project could not have been carried through successfully without the generous financial support of the supporting organisations, whose names are listed prominently at the beginning of this volume, and to which all associated with the volume are deeply grateful. The support of these sponsors – institutions and foundations from four continents – not only acknowledges the international appreciation of Hayek's work, but also provides very tangible evidence of the 'extended order of human cooperation' of which Hayek writes. The Editor also wishes to acknowledge grants in aid of the project from the Werner Erhard Foundation, Sausalito, California, and from the Thyssen Foundation, Cologne, West Germany.

W. W. Bartley, III

xiii

F. A. HAYEK

THE FATAL CONCEIT
The Errors of Socialism

Liberty or Freedom is not, as the origin of the name may seem to
imply, an exemption from all restraints, but rather the most
effectual applications of every just restraint to all members of a
free society whether they be magistrates or subjects.

Adam Ferguson

The rules of morality are not the conclusions of our reason.

David Hume

How can it be that institutions that serve the common welfare
and are extremely significant for its development come into
being without a *common will* directed towards establishing them?

Carl Menger

PREFACE

For this book I adopted two rules. There were to be no footnotes and all arguments not essential to its chief conclusions but of interest or even essential to the specialist were either to be put into smaller print to tell the general reader that he might pass over them without missing points on which the conclusions depended, or else were to be assembled in appendices.

References to works cited or quoted are therefore usually indicated simply by brief statements in brackets of the name of the author (where not clear from the context) and the date of the work, followed after a colon by page numbers where needed. These refer to the list of authorities quoted at the end of the volume. Where a later edition of a work has been used, this is indicated by the latter of the dates given in the form 1786/1973, where the former date refers to the original edition.

It would be impossible to name the obligations one has incurred in the course of a long life of study even if one were to list all the works from which one has acquired one's knowledge and opinions, and still more impossible to list in a bibliography all the works one knows one ought to have studied in order to claim competence in a field as wide as that with which the present work deals. Nor can I hope to list all the personal obligations I have incurred during the many years my efforts were directed towards what was fundamentally the same goal. I wish, however, to express my deep gratitude to Miss Charlotte Cubitt, who has served as my assistant throughout the period that this work was in preparation and without whose dedicated help it never could have been completed; and also to Professor W. W. Bartley, III, of the Hoover Institution, Stanford University, who – when I fell ill for a time, just prior to the completion of the final draft – took this volume in hand and prepared it for the publishers.

F. A. Hayek
Freiburg im Breisgau
April 1988

INTRODUCTION
WAS SOCIALISM A MISTAKE?

> The idea of Socialism is at once grandiose and simple. . . . We may say,
> in fact, that it is one of the most ambitious creations of the human spirit,
> . . . so magnificent, so daring, that it has rightly aroused the greatest
> admiration. If we wish to save the world from barbarism we have to
> refute Socialism, but we cannot thrust it carelessly aside.
>
> Ludwig von Mises

This book argues that our civilisation depends, not only for its origin but
also for its preservation, on what can be precisely described only as the
extended order of human cooperation, an order more commonly, if somewhat misleadingly, known as capitalism. To understand our civilisation,
one must appreciate that the extended order resulted not from human
design or intention but spontaneously: it arose from unintentionally
conforming to certain traditional and largely *moral* practices, many of
which men tend to dislike, whose significance they usually fail to
understand, whose validity they cannot prove, and which have nonetheless fairly rapidly spread by means of an evolutionary selection – the
comparative increase of population and wealth – of those groups that
happened to follow them. The unwitting, reluctant, even painful adoption
of these practices kept these groups together, increased their access to
valuable information of all sorts, and enabled them to be 'fruitful, and
multiply, and replenish the earth, and subdue it' (*Genesis* 1:28). This
process is perhaps the least appreciated facet of human evolution.

Socialists take a different view of these matters. They not only differ
in their conclusions, they see the facts differently. That socialists are
wrong *about the facts* is crucial to my argument, as it will unfold in the
pages that follow. I am prepared to admit that if socialist analyses of the
operation of the existing economic order, and of possible alternatives,
were factually correct, we might be obliged to ensure that the
distribution of incomes conform to certain moral principles, and that
this distribution might be possible only by giving a central authority the
power to direct the use of available resources, and might presuppose the
abolition of individual ownership of means of production. If it were for
instance true that central direction of the means of production could

effect a collective product of at least the same magnitude as that which we now produce, it would indeed prove a grave moral problem how this could be done justly. This, however, is not the position in which we find ourselves. For there is no known way, other than by the distribution of products in a competitive market, to inform individuals in what direction their several efforts must aim so as to contribute as much as possible to the total product.

The main point of my argument is, then, that the conflict between, on one hand, advocates of the spontaneous extended human order created by a competitive market, and on the other hand those who demand a deliberate arrangement of human interaction by central authority based on collective command over available resources is due to a factual error by the latter about how knowledge of these resources is and can be generated and utilised. As a question of fact, this conflict must be settled by scientific study. Such study shows that, by following the spontaneously generated moral traditions underlying the competitive market order (traditions which do not satisfy the canons or norms of rationality embraced by most socialists), we generate and garner greater knowledge and wealth than could ever be obtained or utilised in a centrally-directed economy whose adherents claim to proceed strictly in accordance with 'reason'. Thus socialist aims and programmes are factually impossible to achieve or execute; and they also happen, into the bargain as it were, to be logically impossible.

This is why, contrary to what is often maintained, these matters are not merely ones of differing interests or value judgements. Indeed, the question of how men came to adopt certain values or norms, and what effect these had on the evolution of their civilisation, is itself above all a factual one, one that lies at the heart of the present book, and whose answer is sketched in its first three chapters. The demands of socialism are not moral conclusions derived from the traditions that formed the extended order that made civilisation possible. Rather, they endeavour to overthrow these traditions by a rationally designed moral system whose appeal depends on the instinctual appeal of its promised consequences. They assume that, since people had been able to *generate* some system of rules coordinating their efforts, they must also be able to *design* an even better and more gratifying system. But if humankind owes its very existence to one particular rule-guided form of conduct of proven effectiveness, it simply does not have the option of choosing another merely for the sake of the apparent pleasantness of its immediately visible effects. The dispute between the market order and socialism is no less than a matter of survival. To follow socialist morality would destroy much of present humankind and impoverish much of the rest.

7

All of this raises an important point about which I wish to be explicit from the outset. Although I attack the *presumption* of reason on the part of socialists, my argument is in no way directed against reason properly used. By 'reason properly used' I mean reason that recognises its own limitations and, itself taught by reason, faces the implications of the astonishing fact, revealed by economics and biology, that order generated without design can far outstrip plans men consciously contrive. How, after all, could I be attacking reason in a book arguing that socialism is factually and even logically untenable? Nor do I dispute that reason may, although with caution and in humility, and in a piecemeal way, be directed to the examination, criticism and rejection of traditional institutions and moral principles. This book, like some of my earlier studies, is directed against the traditional norms of reason that guide socialism: norms that I believe embody a naive and uncritical theory of rationality, an obsolete and unscientific methodology that I have elsewhere called 'constructivist rationalism' (1973).

Thus I wish neither to deny reason the power to improve norms and institutions nor even to insist that it is incapable of recasting the whole of our moral system in the direction now commonly conceived as 'social justice'. We can do so, however, only by probing every part of a system of morals. If such a morality pretends to be able to do something that it cannot possibly do, e.g., to fulfill a knowledge-generating and organisational function that is impossible under its own rules and norms, then this impossibility itself provides a decisive rational criticism of that moral system. It is important to confront these consequences, for the notion that, in the last resort, the whole debate is a matter of value judgements and not of facts has prevented professional students of the market order from stressing forcibly enough that socialism cannot possibly do what it promises.

Nor should my argument suggest that I do not share some values widely held by socialists; but I do not believe, as I shall argue later, that the widely held conception of 'social justice' either describes a possible state of affairs or is even meaningful. Neither do I believe, as some proponents of hedonistic ethics recommend, that we can make moral decisions simply by considering the greatest foreseeable gratification.

The starting point for my endeavour might well be David Hume's insight that 'the rules of morality . . . are not conclusions of our reason' (*Treatise*, 1739/1886:II:235). This insight will play a central role in this volume since it frames the basic question it tries to answer – which is *how does our morality emerge, and what implications may its mode of coming into being have for our economic and political life?*

The contention that we are constrained to preserve capitalism because of its superior capacity to utilise dispersed knowledge raises the question of how we came to acquire such an irreplaceable economic order – especially in view of my claim that powerful instinctual and rationalistic impulses rebel against the morals and institutions that capitalism requires.

The answer to this question, sketched in the first three chapters, is built upon the old insight, well known to economics, that our values and institutions are determined not simply by preceding causes but as part of a process of unconscious self-organisation of a structure or pattern. This is true not only of economics, but in a wide area, and is well known today in the biological sciences. This insight was only the first of a growing family of theories that account for the formation of complex structures in terms of processes transcending our capacity to observe all the several circumstances operating in the determination of their particular manifestations. When I began my work I felt that I was nearly alone in working on the evolutionary formation of such highly complex self-maintaining orders. Meanwhile, researches on this kind of problem – under various names, such as autopoiesis, cybernetics, homeostasis, spontaneous order, self-organisation, synergetics, systems theory, and so on – have become so numerous that I have been able to study closely no more than a few of them. This book thus becomes a tributary of a growing stream apparently leading to the gradual development of an evolutionary (but certainly not simply Neo-Darwinian) ethics parallel and supplementary to, yet quite distinct from, the already well-advanced development of evolutionary epistemology.

Though the book raises in this way some difficult scientific and philosophical questions, its chief task remains to demonstrate that one of the most influential political movements of our time, socialism, is based on demonstrably false premises, and despite being inspired by good intentions and led by some of the most intelligent representatives of our time, endangers the standard of living and the life itself of a large proportion of our existing population. This is argued in the fourth through sixth chapters, wherein I examine and refute the socialist challenge to the account of the development and maintenance of our civilisation that I offer in the first three chapters. In the seventh chapter, I turn to our language, to show how it has been debased under socialist influence and how careful we must be to keep ourselves from being seduced by it into socialist ways of thinking. In the eighth chapter, I consider an objection that might be raised not only by socialists, but by others as well: namely, that the population explosion undercuts my argument. Finally, in the ninth chapter, I present briefly a few remarks about the role of religion in the development of our moral traditions.

Since evolutionary theory plays so essential a part in this volume, I should note that one of the promising developments of recent years, leading to a better understanding of the growth and function of knowledge (Popper, 1934/1959), and of complex and spontaneous orders (Hayek, 1964, 1973, 1976, 1979) of various kinds, has been the development of an evolutionary epistemology (Campbell, 1977, 1987; Radnitzky & Bartley, 1987), a theory of knowledge that understands reason and its products as evolutionary developments. In this volume I turn to a set of related problems that, although of great importance, remain largely neglected.

That is, I suggest that we need not only an evolutionary epistemology but also an evolutionary account of moral traditions, and one of a character rather different than hitherto available. Of course the traditional rules of human intercourse, after language, law, markets and money, were the fields in which evolutionary thinking originated. Ethics is the last fortress in which human pride must now bow in recognition of its origins. Such an evolutionary theory of morality is indeed emerging, and its essential insight is that our morals are neither instinctual nor a creation of reason, but constitute a separate tradition – '*between* instinct and reason', as the title of the first chapter indicates – a tradition of staggering importance in enabling us to adapt to problems and circumstances far exceeding our rational capacities. Our moral traditions, like many other aspects of our culture, developed concurrently with our reason, not as its product. Surprising and paradoxical as it may seem to some to say this, these moral traditions outstrip the capacities of reason.

ONE

BETWEEN INSTINCT AND REASON

Consuetudo est quasi altera natura.

Cicero

Les lois de la conscience que nous disons naître de la nature, naissant de la coustume.

M. E. de Montaigne

Zwei Seelen wohnen, ach, in meiner Brust,
Die eine will sich von der anderen trennen.

J. W. von Goethe

Biological and Cultural Evolution

To early thinkers the existence of an order of human activities transcending the vision of an ordering mind seemed impossible. Even Aristotle, who comes fairly late, still believed that order among men could extend only so far as the voice of a herald could reach (*Ethics*, IX, x), and that a state numbering a hundred thousand people was thus impossible. Yet what Aristotle thought impossible had already happened by the time he wrote these words. Despite his achievements as a scientist, Aristotle spoke from his instincts, and not from observation or reflection, when he confined human order to the reach of the herald's cry.

Such beliefs are understandable, for man's instincts, which were fully developed long before Aristotle's time, were not made for the kinds of surroundings, and for the numbers, in which he now lives. They were adapted to life in the small roving bands or troops in which the human race and its immediate ancestors evolved during the few million years while the biological constitution of *homo sapiens* was being formed. These genetically inherited instincts served to steer the cooperation of the members of the troop, a cooperation that was, necessarily, a narrowly circumscribed interaction of fellows known to and trusted by one another. These primitive people were guided by concrete, commonly perceived aims, and by a similar perception of the dangers and opportunities – chiefly sources of food and shelter – of their

11

environment. They not only could *hear* their herald; they usually *knew* him personally.

Although longer experience may have lent some older members of these bands some authority, it was mainly shared aims and perceptions that coordinated the activities of their members. These modes of coordination depended decisively on instincts of solidarity and altruism – instincts applying to the members of one's own group but not to others. The members of these small groups could thus exist only as such: an isolated man would soon have been a dead man. The primitive individualism described by Thomas Hobbes is hence a myth. The savage is not solitary, and his instinct is collectivist. There was never a 'war of all against all'.

Indeed, if our present order did not already exist we too might hardly believe any such thing could ever be possible, and dismiss any report about it as a tale of the miraculous, about what could never come into being. What are chiefly responsible for having generated this extra-ordinary order, and the existence of mankind in its present size and structure, are the rules of human conduct that gradually evolved (especially those dealing with several property, honesty, contract, exchange, trade, competition, gain, and privacy). These rules are handed on by tradition, teaching and imitation, rather than by instinct, and largely consist of prohibitions ('shalt not's') that designate adjustable domains for individual decisions. Mankind achieved civilis-ation by developing and learning to follow rules (first in territorial tribes and then over broader reaches) that often forbade him to do what his instincts demanded, and no longer depended on a common perception of events. These rules, in effect constituting a new and different morality, and to which I would indeed prefer to confine the term 'morality', suppress or restrain the 'natural morality', i.e., those instincts that welded together the small group and secured cooperation within it at the cost of hindering or blocking its expansion.

> I prefer to confine the term 'morality' to those non-instinctive rules that
> enabled mankind to expand into an extended order since the concept of
> morals makes sense only by contrast to impulsive and unreflective conduct
> on one hand, and to rational concern with specific results on the other.
> Innate reflexes have no moral quality, and 'sociobiologists' who apply terms
> like altruism to them (and who should, to be consistent, regard copulation as
> the most altruistic) are plainly wrong. Only if we mean to say that we *ought*
> to follow 'altruistic' emotions does altruism become a moral concept.
>   Admittedly, this is hardly the only way to use these terms. Bernard
> Mandeville scandalized his contemporaries by arguing that 'the grand
> principle that makes us social creatures, the solid basis, the life and support

12

of all trade and employment without exception' is *evil* (1715/1924), by which he meant, precisely, that the rules of the extended order conflicted with innate instincts that had bound the small group together.

Once we view morals not as innate instincts but as learnt traditions, their relation to what we ordinarily call feelings, emotions or sentiments raises various interesting questions. For instance, although learnt, morals do not necessarily always operate as explicit rules, but may manifest themselves, as do true instincts, as vague disinclinations to, or distastes for, certain kinds of action. Often they tell us how to choose among, or to avoid, inborn instinctual drives.

It may be asked how restraints on instinctual demands serve to coordinate the activities of larger numbers. As an example, continued obedience to the command to treat all men as neighbours would have prevented the growth of an extended order. For those now living within the extended order gain from *not* treating one another as neighbours, and by applying, in their interactions, rules of the extended order – such as those of several property and contract – instead of the rules of solidarity and altruism. An order in which everyone treated his neighbour as himself would be one where comparatively few could be fruitful and multiply. If we were, say, to respond to all charitable appeals that bombard us through the media, this would exact a heavy cost in distracting us from what we are most competent to do, and likely only make us the tools of particular interest groups or of peculiar views of the relative importance of particular needs. It would not provide a proper cure for misfortunes about which we are understandably concerned. Similarly, instinctual aggressiveness towards outsiders must be curbed if identical abstract rules are to apply to the relations of all men, and thus to reach across boundaries – even the boundaries of states.

Thus, forming superindividual patterns or systems of cooperation required individuals to change their 'natural' or 'instinctual' responses to others, something strongly resisted. That such conflicts with inborn instincts, 'private vices', as Bernard Mandeville described them, might turn out to be 'public benefits', and that men had to restrain some 'good' instincts in order to develop the extended order, are conclusions that became the source of dissension later too. For example, Rousseau took the side of the 'natural' although his contemporary Hume clearly saw that 'so noble an affection [as generosity] instead of fitting men for large societies, is almost as contrary to them, as the most narrow selfishness' (1739/1886:II, 270).

Constraints on the practices of the small group, it must be emphasised and repeated, are *hated*. For, as we shall see, the individual following them, even though he depend on them for life, does not and usually cannot understand how they function or how they benefit him. He knows so many objects that seem desirable but for which he is not permitted to grasp, and he cannot see how other beneficial features of his environment depend on the discipline to which he is forced to submit – a discipline forbidding him to reach out for these same appealing objects. Disliking these constraints so much, we hardly can be said to have selected them; rather, these constraints selected us: they enabled us to survive.

It is no accident that many abstract rules, such as those treating individual responsibility and several property, are associated with economics. Economics has from its origins been concerned with how an extended order of human interaction comes into existence through a process of variation, winnowing and sifting far surpassing our vision or our capacity to design. Adam Smith was the first to perceive that we have stumbled upon methods of ordering human economic cooperation that exceed the limits of our knowledge and perception. His 'invisible hand' had perhaps better have been described as an invisible or unsurveyable pattern. We are led – for example by the pricing system in market exchange – to do things by circumstances of which we are largely unaware and which produce results that we do not intend. In our economic activities we do not know the needs which we satisfy nor the sources of the things which we get. Almost all of us serve people whom we do not know, and even of whose existence we are ignorant; and we in turn constantly live on the services of other people of whom we know nothing. All this is possible because we stand in a great framework of institutions and traditions – economic, legal, and moral – into which we fit ourselves by obeying certain rules of conduct that we never made, and which we have never understood in the sense in which we understand how the things that we manufacture function.

Modern economics explains how such an extended order can come into being, and how it itself constitutes an information-gathering process, able to call up, and to put to use, widely dispersed information that no central planning agency, let alone any individual, could know as a whole, possess or control. Man's knowledge, as Smith knew, is dispersed. As he wrote, 'What is the species of domestic industry his capital can employ, and of which the produce is likely to be of the greatest value, every individual, it is evident, in his local situation, judges much better than any statesman or lawgiver can do for him' (1776/1976:II, 487). Or as an acute economic thinker of the nineteenth century put it, economic enterprise requires 'minute knowledge of a thousand particulars which will be learnt by nobody but him who has an interest in knowing them' (Bailey, 1840:3). Information-gathering institutions such as the market enable us to use such dispersed and unsurveyable knowledge to form super-individual patterns. After institutions and traditions based on such patterns evolved, it was no longer necessary for people to strive for agreement on a unitary purpose (as in the small band), for widely dispersed knowledge and skills could now readily be brought into play for diverse ends.

This development is readily apparent in biology as well as in economics. Even within biology in the strict sense 'evolutionary change in general tends towards a maximum economy in the use of resources' and 'evolution thus "blindly" follows the route of maximum resources use' (Howard, 1982:83). Further, a modern biologist has rightly observed that 'ethics is the study of the way to allocate resources' (Hardin, 1980:3) – all of which points to the close interconnections among evolution, biology, and ethics.

The concept of order is difficult – like its near equivalents 'system', 'structure' and 'pattern'. We need to distinguish two different but related conceptions of order. As a verb or noun, 'order' may be used to describe *either* the results of a *mental* activity of arranging or classifying objects or events in various aspects according to our sense perception, as the scientific re-arrangement of the sensory world tells us to do (Hayek, 1952), *or* as the particular *physical* arrangements that objects or events either are supposed to possess or which are attributed to them at a certain time. Regularity, derived from the Latin *regula* for rule, and order are of course simply the temporal and the spatial aspects of the same sort of relation between elements.

Bearing this distinction in mind, we may say that humans acquired the ability to bring about factually ordered arrangements serving their needs because they learned to order the sensory stimuli from their surroundings according to several different principles, rearrangements *superimposed over* the order or classification effected by their senses and instincts. Ordering in the sense of classifying objects and events is a way of actively rearranging them to produce desired results.

We learn to classify objects chiefly through language, with which we not merely label known kinds of objects but specify what *we are to regard* as objects or events of the same or different kinds. We also learn from custom, morality and law about effects expected from different kinds of action. For example, the values or prices formed by interaction in markets prove to be further superimposed means of classifying kinds of actions according to the significance they have for an order of which the individual is merely one element in a whole which he never made.

The extended order did not of course arise all at once; the process lasted longer and produced a greater variety of forms than its eventual development into a world-wide civilisation might suggest (taking perhaps hundreds of thousands of years rather than five or six thousand); and the market order is comparatively late. The various structures, traditions, institutions and other components of this order arose gradually as variations of habitual modes of conduct were selected. Such new rules would spread not because men understood that they were more effective, or could calculate that they would lead to expansion, but simply because they enabled those groups practising them to procreate more successfully and to include outsiders.

This evolution came about, then, through the spreading of new practices by a process of transmission of acquired habits analogous to, but also in important respects different from, biological evolution. I shall consider some of these analogies and differences below, but we might mention here that biological evolution would have been far too slow to alter or replace man's innate responses in the course of the ten or twenty thousand years during which civilisation has developed – not to speak of being too slow to have influenced the far greater numbers whose ancestors joined the process only a few hundred years ago. Yet so far as we know, all currently civilised groups appear to possess a similar capacity for acquiring civilisation by learning certain traditions. Thus it hardly seems possible that civilisation and culture are genetically determined and transmitted. They have to be learnt by all alike through tradition.

The earliest clear statement of such matters known to me was made by A. M. Carr-Saunders who wrote that 'man and groups are naturally selected on account of the customs they practice just as they are selected on account of their mental and physical characters. Those groups practising the most advantageous customs will have an advantage in the constant struggle between adjacent groups over those that practise less advantageous customs' (1922:223, 302). Carr-Saunders, however, stressed the capacity to restrict rather than to increase population. For more recent studies see Alland (1967); Farb (1968:13); Simpson, who described culture, as opposed to biology, as 'the more powerful means of adaptation' (in B. Campbell, 1972); Popper, who argued that 'cultural evolution continues genetic evolution by other means' (Popper and Eccles, 1977:48); and Durham (in Chagnon and Irons, 1979:19), who emphasises the effect of particular customs and attributes in enhancing human reproduction.

This gradual replacement of innate responses by learnt rules increasingly distinguished man from other animals, although the propensity to instinctive mass action remains one of several beastly characteristics that man has retained (Trotter, 1916). Even man's animal ancestors had already acquired certain 'cultural' traditions before they became, anatomically, modern man. Such cultural traditions have also helped to shape some animal societies, as among birds and apes, and probably also among many other mammals (Bonner, 1980). Yet the decisive change from animal to man was due to such culturally-determined restraints on innate responses.

Whilst learnt rules, which the individual came to obey habitually and almost as unconsciously as inherited instincts, increasingly replaced the latter, we cannot precisely distinguish between these two determinants of conduct because they interact in complicated ways. Practices learnt as infants have become as much part of our personalities as what governed us already when we began to learn. Even some structural changes in the human body have occurred because they helped man to take fuller advantage of opportunities provided by cultural developments. Neither is it important for our present purposes how much of the abstract structure that we call mind is transmitted genetically and embodied in the physical structure of our central nervous system, or how far it serves only as a receptacle enabling us to absorb cultural tradition. The results of genetic and cultural transmission may both be called traditions. What is important is that the two often conflict in the ways mentioned.

Not even the near universality of some cultural attributes proves that they are genetically determined. There may exist just one way to satisfy certain requirements for forming an extended order – just as the development of wings is apparently the only way in which organisms can become able to fly (the wings of insects, birds and bats have quite different genetic origins). There may also be fundamentally only one way to develop a phonetic language, so that the existence of certain common attributes possessed by all languages also does not by itself show that they must be due to innate qualities.

Two Moralities in Cooperation and Conflict

Although cultural evolution, and the civilisation that it created, brought differentiation, individualisation, increasing wealth, and great expansion to mankind, its gradual advent has been far from smooth. We have not shed our heritage from the face-to-face troop, nor have these instincts either 'adjusted' fully to our relatively new extended order or been rendered harmless by it.

Yet the lasting benefits of some instincts should not be overlooked,

17

including the particular endowment that enabled some other instinctual modes to be at least partly displaced. For example, by the time culture began to displace some innate modes of behaviour, genetic evolution had probably also already endowed human individuals with a great variety of characteristics which were better adjusted to the many different environmental niches into which men had penetrated than those of any non-domesticated animal – and this was probably so even before growing division of labour within groups provided new chances of survival for special types. Among the most important of these innate characteristics which helped to displace other instincts was a great capacity for learning from one's fellows, especially by imitation. The prolongation of infancy and adolescence, which contributed to this capacity, was probably the last decisive step determined by biological evolution.

Moreover, the structures of the extended order are made up not only of individuals but also of many, often overlapping, sub-orders within which old instinctual responses, such as solidarity and altruism, continue to retain some importance by assisting voluntary collaboration, even though they are incapable, by themselves, of creating a basis for the more extended order. Part of our present difficulty is that we must constantly adjust our lives, our thoughts and our emotions, in order to live simultaneously within different kinds of orders according to different rules. If we were to apply the unmodified, uncurbed, rules of the micro-cosmos (i.e., of the small band or troop, or of, say, our families) to the macro-cosmos (our wider civilisation), as our instincts and sentimental yearnings often make us wish to do, *we would destroy it*. Yet if we were always to apply the rules of the extended order to our more intimate groupings, *we would crush them*. So we must learn to live in two sorts of world at once. To apply the name 'society' to both, or even to either, is hardly of any use, and can be most misleading (see chapter seven).

Yet despite the advantages attending our limited ability to live simultaneously within *two* orders of rules, and to distinguish between them, it is anything but easy to do either. Indeed, our instincts often threaten to topple the whole edifice. The topic of this book thus resembles, in a way, that of *Civilisation and Its Discontents* (1930), except that my conclusions differ greatly from Freud's. Indeed, the conflict between what men instinctively like and the learnt rules of conduct that enabled them to expand – a conflict fired by the discipline of 'repressive or inhibitory moral traditions', as D. T. Campbell calls it – is perhaps the major theme of the history of civilisation. It seems that Columbus recognised at once that the life of the 'savages' whom he encountered was more gratifying to innate human instincts. And as I shall argue later, I believe that an atavistic longing after the life of the noble savage is the main source of the collectivist tradition.

Natural Man Unsuited to the Extended Order

One can hardly expect people either to like an extended order that runs counter to some of their strongest instincts, or readily to understand that it brings them the material comforts they also want. The order is even 'unnatural' in the common meaning of not conforming to man's biological endowment. Much of the good that man does in the extended order is thus not due to his being naturally good; yet it is foolish to deprecate civilisation as artificial for this reason. It is artificial only in the sense in which most of our values, our language, our art and our very reason are artificial: they are not genetically embedded in our biological structures. In another sense, however, the extended order is perfectly natural: in the sense that it has itself, like similar biological phenomena, evolved naturally in the course of natural selection (see Appendix A).

Nonetheless it is true that the greater part of our daily lives, and the pursuit of most occupations, give little satisfaction to deep-seated 'altruistic' desires to do visible good. Rather, accepted practices often require us to leave undone what our instincts impel us to do. It is not so much, as is often suggested, emotion and reason that conflict, but innate instincts and learnt rules. Yet, as we shall see, following these learnt rules generally does have the effect of providing a greater benefit to the community at large than most direct 'altruistic' action that a particular individual might take.

One revealing mark of how poorly the ordering principle of the market is understood is the common notion that 'cooperation is better than competition'. Cooperation, like solidarity, presupposes a large measure of agreement on ends as well as on methods employed in their pursuit. It makes sense in a small group whose members share particular habits, knowledge and beliefs about possibilities. It makes hardly any sense when the problem is to adapt to unknown circumstances; yet it is this adaptation to the unknown on which the coordination of efforts in the extended order rests. Competition is a procedure of discovery, a procedure involved in all evolution, that led man unwittingly to respond to novel situations; and through further competition, not through agreement, we gradually increase our efficiency.

To operate beneficially, competition requires that those involved observe rules rather than resort to physical force. Rules alone can unite an extended order. (Common ends can do so only during a temporary emergency that creates a common danger for all. The 'moral equivalent of war' offered to evoke solidarity is but a relapse into cruder principles of coordination.) Neither all ends pursued, nor all means used, are known or need to be known to anybody, in order for them to be taken account of within a spontaneous order. Such an order forms of itself. That rules become increasingly better adjusted to generate order happened not because men better understood their function, but because those groups prospered who happened to change them in a way that rendered them increasingly adaptive. This evolution was not linear, but resulted from continued trial and error, constant 'experimentation' in arenas wherein different orders contended. Of course there was no intention to experiment – yet the changes in rules thrown forth by historical accident, analogous to genetic mutations, had something of the same effect.

The evolution of rules was far from unhindered, since the powers enforcing the rules generally resisted rather than assisted changes conflicting with traditional views about what was right or just. In turn, enforcement of newly learnt rules that had fought their way to acceptance sometimes blocked the next step of evolution, or restricted a further extension of the coordination of individual efforts. Coercive authority has rarely initiated such extensions of coordination, though it has from time to time spread a morality that had already gained acceptance within a ruling group.

All this confirms that the feelings that press against the restraints of civilisation are anachronistic, adapted to the size and conditions of groups in the distant past. Moreover, if civilisation has resulted from unwanted gradual changes in morality, then, reluctant as we may be to accept this, no universally valid system of ethics can ever be known to us.

It would however be wrong to conclude, strictly from such evolutionary premises, that whatever rules have evolved are always or necessarily conducive to the survival and increase of the populations following them. We need to show, with the help of economic analysis (see chapter five), how rules that emerge spontaneously tend to promote human survival. Recognising that rules generally tend to be selected, via competition, on the basis of their human survival-value certainly does not protect those rules from critical scrutiny. This is so, if for no other reason, because there has so often been coercive interference in the process of cultural evolution.

Yet an understanding of cultural evolution will indeed tend to shift the benefit of the doubt to established rules, and to place the burden of proof on those wishing to reform them. While it cannot prove the superiority of market institutions, a historical and evolutionary survey of the emergence of capitalism (such as that presented in chapters two and three) helps to explain how such productive, albeit unpopular and unintended, traditions happened to emerge, and how deep is their significance for those immersed in the extended order. First, however, I want to remove from the path just outlined a major stumbling-block, in the form of a widely shared misconception of the nature of our capacity to adopt useful practices.

Mind Is Not a Guide but a Product of Cultural Evolution, and Is Based More on Imitation than on Insight or Reason

We have mentioned the capacity to learn by imitation as one of the prime benefits conferred during our long instinctual development. Indeed, perhaps the most important capacity with which the human individual is genetically endowed, beyond innate responses, is his ability to acquire skills by largely imitative learning. In view of this, it is important to avoid, right from the start, a notion that stems from what I call the 'fatal conceit': the idea that the ability to acquire skills stems from reason. For it is the other way around: our reason is as much the result of an evolutionary selection process as is our morality. It stems however from a somewhat separate development, so that one should never suppose that our reason is in the higher critical position and that only those moral rules are valid that reason endorses.

I shall examine these matters in subsequent chapters, but a foretaste of my conclusions may be in place here. The title of the present chapter, 'Between Instinct and Reason', is meant literally. I want to call attention to what does indeed lie *between* instinct and reason, and which on that account is often overlooked just because it is assumed that there is nothing between the two. That is, I am chiefly concerned with cultural and moral evolution, evolution of the extended order, which is, on the one hand (as we have just seen), beyond instinct and often opposed to it, and which is, on the other hand (as we shall see later), incapable of being created or designed by reason.

My views, some of which have been sketched earlier (1952/79, 1973, 1976, 1979), can be summarised simply. Learning how to behave is more the *source* than the *result* of insight, reason, and understanding. Man is not born wise, rational and good, but has to be taught to become so. It is not our intellect that created our morals; rather, human interactions governed by our morals make possible the growth of reason and those capabilities associated with it. Man became intelligent because there was *tradition* – that which lies between instinct and reason – for him to learn. This tradition, in turn, originated not from a

21

capacity rationally to interpret observed facts but from habits of responding. It told man primarily what he ought or ought not to do under certain conditions rather than what he must expect to happen.

Thus I confess that I always have to smile when books on evolution, even ones written by great scientists, end, as they often do, with exhortations which, while conceding that everything has hitherto developed by a process of spontaneous order, call on human reason – now that things have become so complex – to seize the reins and control future development. Such wishful thinking is encouraged by what I have elsewhere called the 'constructivist rationalism' (1973) that affects much scientific thinking, and which was made quite explicit in the title of a highly successful book by a well-known socialist anthropologist, *Man Makes Himself* (V. Gordon Childe, 1936), a title that was adopted by many socialists as a sort of watchword (Heilbroner, 1970:106). These assumptions include the unscientific, even animistic, notion that at some stage the rational human mind or soul entered the evolving human body and became a new, active guide of further cultural development (rather than, as actually happened, that this body gradually acquired the capacity to absorb exceedingly complex principles that enabled it to move more successfully in its own environment). This notion that cultural evolution entirely postdates biological or genetic evolution passes over the most important part of the evolutionary process, that in which reason itself was formed. The idea that reason, itself created in the course of evolution, should now be in a position to determine its own future evolution (not to mention any number of other things which it is also incapable of doing) is inherently contradictory, and can readily be refuted (see chapters five and six). It is less accurate to suppose that thinking man creates and controls his cultural evolution than it is to say that culture, and evolution, created his reason. In any case, the idea that at some point conscious design stepped in and displaced evolution substitutes a virtually supernatural postulate for scientific explanation. So far as scientific explanation is concerned, it was not what we know as mind that developed civilisation, let alone directed its evolution, but rather mind and civilisation which developed or evolved concurrently. What we call mind is not something that the individual is born with, as he is born with his brain, or something that the brain produces, but something that his genetic equipment (e.g., a brain of a certain size and structure) helps him to acquire, as he grows up, from his family and adult fellows by absorbing the results of a tradition that is not genetically transmitted. Mind in this sense consists less of testable knowledge about the world, less in interpretations of man's surroundings, more in the capacity to restrain instincts – a capacity which cannot be tested by individual reason since

22

its effects are on the group. Shaped by the environment in which individuals grow up, mind in turn conditions the preservation, development, richness, and variety of traditions on which individuals draw. By being transmitted largely through families, mind preserves a multiplicity of concurrent streams into which each newcomer to the community can delve. It may well be asked whether an individual who did not have the opportunity to tap such a cultural tradition could be said even to have a mind.

Just as instinct is older than custom and tradition, so then are the latter older than reason: custom and tradition stand *between* instinct and reason – logically, psychologically, temporally. They are due neither to what is sometimes called the unconscious, nor to intuition, nor to rational understanding. Though in a sense based on human experience in that they were shaped in the course of cultural evolution, they were not formed by drawing reasoned conclusions from certain facts or from an awareness that things behaved in a particular way. Though governed in our conduct by what we have learnt, we often do not know why we do what we do. Learnt moral rules, customs, progressively displaced innate responses, not because men recognised by reason that they were better but because they made possible the growth of an extended order exceeding anyone's vision, in which more effective collaboration enabled its members, however blindly, to maintain more people and to displace other groups.

The Mechanism of Cultural Evolution Is Not Darwinian

We are led by our argument to consider more closely the relationship between the theory of evolution and the development of culture. It is an issue that raises a number of interesting questions, to many of which economics provides an access that few other disciplines offer.

There has however been great confusion about the matter, some of which should be mentioned if only to warn the reader that we do not intend to repeat it here. Social Darwinism, in particular, proceeded from the assumption that any investigator into the evolution of human culture has to go to school with Darwin. This is mistaken. I have the greatest admiration for Charles Darwin as the first who succeeded in elaborating a consistent (if still incomplete) theory of evolution in any field. Yet his painstaking efforts to illustrate how the process of evolution operated in living organisms convinced the scientific community of what had long been a commonplace in the humanities – at least since Sir William Jones in 1787 recognised the striking resemblance of Latin and Greek to Sanskrit, and the descent of all 'Indo-Germanic' languages from the latter. This example reminds us that the Darwinian or biological theory of evolution was neither the first nor the only such theory, and actually is wholly distinct, and differs somewhat from, other evolutionary accounts. The idea of biological evolution stems from the study of processes of cultural development which had been recognised earlier: processes that lead to the formulation of institutions like language (as in the work of Jones), law, morals, markets, and money.

> Thus perhaps the chief error of contemporary 'sociobiology' is to suppose that language, morals, law, and such like, are transmitted by the 'genetic' processes that molecular biology is now illuminating, rather than being the products of selective evolution transmitted by imitative learning. This idea is as wrong – although at the other end of the spectrum – as the notion that man consciously invented or designed institutions like morals, law, language or money, and thus can improve them at will, a notion that is a remnant of the superstition that evolutionary theory in biology had to combat: namely, that wherever we find order there must have been a personal orderer. Here again we find that an accurate account lies *between* instinct and reason.

Not only is the idea of evolution older in the humanities and social sciences than in the natural sciences, I would even be prepared to argue that Darwin got the basic ideas of evolution from economics. As we learn from his notebooks, Darwin was reading Adam Smith just when, in 1838, he was formulating his own theory (see Appendix A below).[1] In any case, Darwin's work was preceded by decades, indeed by a century, of research concerning the rise of highly complex spontaneous orders through a process of evolution. Even words like 'genetic' and 'genetics', which have today become technical expressions of biology, were by no means invented by biologists. The first person I know to have spoken of genetic development was the German philosopher and cultural historian Herder. We find the idea again in Wieland, and again in Humboldt. Thus modern biology has borrowed the concept of evolution from studies of culture of older lineage. If this is in a sense

---

[1] See Howard E. Gruber, *Darwin on Man: A Psychological Study of Scientific Creativity, together with Darwin's Early and Unpublished Notebooks*, transcribed and annotated by Paul H. Barrett (New York: E. P. Dutton & Co., Inc., 1974), pp. 13, 57, 302, 305, 321, 360, 380. In 1838 Darwin read Smith's *Essays on Philosophical Subjects*, to which was prefixed Dugald Stewart's *An Account of the Life and Writings of the Author* (London: Cadell and Davies, 1795, pp. xxvi–xxvii). Of the latter, Darwin noted that he had read it and that it was 'worth reading as giving abstract of Smith's views'. In 1839 Darwin read Smith's *The Theory of Moral Sentiments; or, An Essay Towards an Analysis of the Principles by which Men Naturally judge concerning the Conduct and Character, first of their Neighbours, and afterwards of themselves, to which is added, A Dissertation on the Origin of Languages*, 10th ed., 2 vols. (London: Cadell & Davies, 1804). There does not appear to be any evidence that Darwin read *The Wealth of Nations*. – Ed.

24

well known, it is also almost always forgotten.

Of course the theory of cultural evolution (sometimes also described as psycho-social, super-organic, or exosomatic evolution) and the theory of biological evolution are, although analogous in some important ways, hardly identical. Indeed, they often start from quite different assumptions. Cultural evolution is, as Julian Huxley justly stated, 'a process differing radically from biological evolution, with its own laws and mechanisms and modalities, and not capable of explanation on purely biological grounds' (Huxley, 1947). Just to mention several important differences: although biological theory now excludes the inheritance of acquired characteristics, all cultural development rests on such inheritance – characteristics in the form of rules guiding the mutual relations among individuals which are not innate but learnt. To refer to terms now used in biological discussion, cultural evolution *simulates* Lamarckism (Popper, 1972). *Moreover,* cultural evolution is brought about through transmission of habits and information not merely from the individual's physical parents, but from an indefinite number of 'ancestors'. The processes furthering the transmission and spreading of cultural properties by learning also, as already noted, make cultural evolution incomparably faster than biological evolution. Finally, cultural evolution operates largely through group selection; whether group selection also operates in biological evolution remains an open question – one on which my argument does not depend (Edelman, 1987; Ghiselin, 1969:57–9, 132–3; Hardy, 1965:153ff, 206; Mayr, 1970:114; Medawar, 1983:134–5; Ruse, 1982:190–5, 203–6, 235–6).

> It is wrong for Bonner (1980:10) to claim that culture is 'as biological as any other function of an organism, for instance respiration or locomotion'. To label 'biological' the formation of the tradition of language, morals, law, money, even of the mind, abuses language and misunderstands theory. Our genetic inheritance may determine what we are capable of learning but certainly not what tradition is there to learn. What is there to learn is not even the product of the human brain. What is not transmitted by genes is not a biological phenomenon.

Despite such differences, all evolution, cultural as well as biological, is a process of continuous adaptation to unforeseeable events, to contingent circumstances which could not have been forecast. This is another reason why evolutionary theory can never put us in the position of rationally predicting and controlling future evolution. All it can do is to show how complex structures carry within themselves a means of correction that leads to further evolutionary developments which are, however, in accordance with their very nature, themselves unavoidably unpredictable.

25

Having mentioned several differences between cultural and biological evolution, I should stress that in one important respect they are at one: neither biological nor cultural evolution knows anything like 'laws of evolution' or 'inevitable laws of historical development' in the sense of laws governing necessary stages or phases through which the products of evolution must pass, and enabling the prediction of future developments. Cultural evolution is determined neither genetically nor otherwise, and its results are diversity, not uniformity. Those philosophers like Marx and Auguste Comte who have contended that our studies can lead to laws of evolution enabling the prediction of inevitable future developments are mistaken. In the past, evolutionary approaches to ethics have been discredited chiefly because evolution was wrongly connected with such alleged 'laws of evolution', whereas in fact the theory of evolution must emphatically repudiate such laws as impossible. As I have argued elsewhere (1952), complex phenomena are confined to what I call pattern prediction or predictions of the principle.

One of the main sources of this particular misunderstanding results from confusing two wholly different processes which biologists distinguish as *ontogenetic* and *phylogenetic*. Ontogenesis has to do with the predetermined development of individuals, something indeed set by inherent mechanisms built into the genom of the germ cell. By contrast, phylogeny – that with which evolution is concerned – deals with the evolutionary history of the species or type. While biologists have generally been protected against confusing these two by their training, students of affairs unfamiliar with biology often fall victim to their ignorance and are led to 'historicist' beliefs that imply that phylogenesis operates in the same way as does ontogenesis. These historicist notions were effectively refuted by Sir Karl Popper (1945, 1957).

Biological and cultural evolution share other features too. For example, they both rely on the same principle of selection: survival or reproductive advantage. Variation, adaptation and competition are essentially the same kind of process, however different their particular mechanisms, particularly those pertaining to propagation. Not only does all evolution rest on competition; continuing competition is necessary even to preserve existing achievements.

Although I wish the theory of evolution to be seen in its broad historical setting, the differences between biological and cultural evolution to be understood, and the contribution of the social sciences to our knowledge of evolution to be recognized, I do not wish to dispute that the working out of Darwin's theory of biological evolution, in all of its ramifications, is one of the great intellectual achievements of modern times – one that gives us a completely new view of our world. Its universality as a means

26

of explanation is also expressed in the new work of some distinguished physical scientists, which shows that the idea of evolution is in no way limited to organisms, but rather that it begins in a sense already with atoms, which have developed out of more elementary particles, and that we can thus explain molecules, the most primitive complex organisms, and even the complex modern world through various processes of evolution (see Appendix A).

No one who takes an evolutionary approach to the study of culture can, however, fail to be aware of the hostility often shown towards such approaches. Such hostility often stems from reactions to just those 'social scientists' who in the nineteenth century needed Darwin to recognise what they ought to have learnt from their own predecessors, and who did a lasting disservice to the advance of the theory of cultural evolution, which they indeed brought into discredit.

Social Darwinism is wrong in many respects, but the intense dislike of it shown today is also partly due to its conflicting with the fatal conceit that man is able to shape the world around him according to his wishes. Although this too has nothing to do with evolutionary theory properly understood, constructivist students of human affairs often use the inappropriateness (and such plain mistakes) of Social Darwinism as a pretext for rejecting any evolutionary approach at all.

Bertrand Russell provides a good example in his claim that 'if evolutionary ethics were sound, we ought to be entirely indifferent to what the course of evolution might be, since whatever it is is thereby proved to be best' (1910/1966:24). This objection, which A.G.N. Flew (1967:48) regards as 'decisive', rests on a simple misunderstanding. I have no intention to commit what is often called the genetic or naturalistic fallacy. I do not claim that the results of group selection of traditions are necessarily 'good' – any more than I claim that other things that have long survived in the course of evolution, such as cockroaches, have moral value.

I do claim that, whether we like it or not, without the particular traditions I have mentioned, the extended order of civilisation could not continue to exist (whereas, were cockroaches to disappear, the resulting ecological 'disaster' would perhaps not wreak permanent havoc on mankind); and that if we discard these traditions, out of ill-considered notions (which may indeed genuinely commit the naturalistic fallacy) of what it is to be reasonable, we shall doom a large part of mankind to poverty and death. Only when these facts are fully faced do we have any business – or are we likely to have any competence – to consider what the right and good thing to do may be.

While facts alone can never determine what is right, ill-considered notions of what is reasonable, right and good may change the facts and

27

the circumstances in which we live; they may destroy, perhaps forever, not only developed individuals and buildings and art and cities (which we have long known to be vulnerable to the destructive powers of moralities and ideologies of various sorts), but also traditions, institutions, and interrelations without which such creations could hardly have come into being or ever be recreated.

TWO

THE ORIGINS OF LIBERTY,
PROPERTY AND JUSTICE

Nobody is at liberty to attack several property and to say that he values
civilisation. The history of the two cannot be disentangled.

Henry Sumner Maine

Property . . . is therefore inseparable from human economy in its social
form.

Carl Menger

Men are qualified for civil liberties, in exact proportion to their
disposition to put moral chains upon their appetites: in proportion as
their love of justice is above their rapacity.

Edmund Burke

Freedom and the Extended Order

If morals and tradition, rather than intelligence and calculating reason,
lifted men above the savages, the distinctive foundations of modern
civilisation were laid in antiquity in the region surrounding the
Mediterranean Sea. There, possibilities of long-distance trade gave, to
those communities whose individuals were allowed to make free use of
their individual knowledge, an advantage over those in which common
local knowledge or that of a ruler determined the activities of all. So far
as we know, the Mediterranean region was the first to see the
acceptance of a person's right to dispose over a recognised private
domain, thus allowing individuals to develop a dense network of
commercial relations among different communities. Such a network
worked independently of the views and desires of local chiefs, for the
movements of naval traders could hardly be centrally directed in those
days. If we may accept the account of a highly respected authority (and
one certainly not biased in favour of the market order), 'the
Graeco–Roman world was essentially and precisely one of private
ownership, whether of a few acres or of the enormous domains of
Roman senators and emperors, a world of private trade and
manufacture' (Finley, 1973:29).

Such an order serving a multiplicity of private purposes could in fact have been formed only on the basis of what I prefer to call *several property*, which is H. S. Maine's more precise term for what is usually described as private property. If several property is the heart of the morals of any advanced civilisation, the ancient Greeks seem to have been the first to see that it is also inseparable from individual freedom. The makers of the constitution of ancient Crete are reported to have 'taken it for granted that liberty is a state's highest good and for this reason alone make property belong specifically to those who acquire it, whereas in a condition of slavery everything belongs to the rulers' (Strabo, 10, 4, 16).

An important aspect of this freedom – the freedom on the part of different individuals or sub-groups to pursue distinct aims, guided by their differing knowledge and skills – was made possible not only by the separate control of various means of production, but also by another practice, virtually inseparable from the first: the recognition of approved methods of transferring this control. The individual's ability to decide for himself how to use specific things, being guided by his own knowledge and expectations as well as by those of whatever group he might join, depends on general recognition of a respected private domain of which the individual is free to dispose, and an equally recognised way in which the right to particular things can be transferred from one person to another. The prerequisite for the existence of such property, freedom, and order, from the time of the Greeks to the present, is the same: law in the sense of abstract rules enabling any individual to ascertain at any time who is entitled to dispose over any particular thing.

With respect to some objects, the notion of individual property must have appeared very early, and the first hand-crafted tools are perhaps an appropriate example. The attachment of a unique and highly useful tool or weapon to its maker might, however, be so strong that transfer became so psychologically difficult that the instrument must accompany him even into the grave – as in the *tholos* or beehive tombs of the Mycenaean period. Here the fusion of inventor with 'rightful owner' appears, and with it numerous elaborations of the basic idea, sometimes accompanied also by legend, as in the later story of Arthur and his sword Excalibur – a story in which the transfer of the sword came about *not* by human law but by a 'higher' law of magic or 'the powers'.

The extension and refinement of the concept of property were, as such examples suggest, necessarily gradual processes that are hardly completed even today. Such a concept cannot yet have been of much significance in the roving bands of hunters and gatherers among whom the discoverer of a source of food or place of shelter was obliged to reveal his find to his fellows. The first individually crafted durable tools probably became attached to their makers because they were the only ones who had the skill to use them – and here again the story of Arthur and Excalibur is appropriate, for while Arthur did not make Excalibur, he was the only one able to use it. Separate ownership of perishable goods, on the other hand, may have appeared only later as the solidarity of the group weakened and individuals became responsible for more limited groups such as the family. Probably the need to keep a workable holding intact gradually led from group ownership to individual property in land.

There is however little use in speculating about the particular sequence of these developments, for they probably varied considerably among the peoples who progressed through nomadic herding and those who developed agriculture. The crucial point is that the prior development of several property is indispensable for the development of trading, and thereby for the formation of larger coherent and cooperating structures, and for the appearance of those signals we call prices. Whether individuals, or extended families, or voluntary groupings of individuals were recognised as owning particular objects is less important than that all were permitted to choose which individuals would determine what use was to be made of their property. There will also have developed, especially with regard to land, such arrangements as 'vertical' division of property rights between superior and inferior owners, or ultimate owners and lessees, such as are used in modern estate developments, of which more use could perhaps be made today than some more primitive conceptions of property allow.

Nor should tribes be thought of as the stock from which cultural evolution began; they are, rather, its earliest product. These 'earliest' coherent groups were of common descent and community of practice with other groups and individuals with whom they were not necessarily familiar (as will be discussed in the next chapter). Hence we can hardly say when tribes first appeared as preservers of shared traditions, and cultural evolution began. Yet somehow, however slowly, however marked by setbacks, orderly cooperation was extended, and common concrete ends were replaced by general, end-independent abstract rules of conduct.

The Classical Heritage of European Civilisation

It appears also to have been the Greeks, and especially the Stoic philosophers, with their cosmopolitan outlook, who first formulated the moral tradition which the Romans later propagated throughout their Empire. That this tradition arouses great resistance we already know and will witness again repeatedly. In Greece it was of course chiefly the

Spartans, the people who resisted the commercial revolution most strongly, who did not recognise individual property but allowed and even encouraged theft. To our time they have remained the prototype of savages who rejected civilisation (for representative 18th-century views on them compare Dr. Samuel Johnson in Boswell's *Life* or Friedrich Schiller's essay *Über die Gesetzgebung des Lykurgos und Solon*). Yet already in Plato and Aristotle, however, we find a nostalgic longing for return to Spartan practice, and this longing persists to the present. It is a craving for a micro-order determined by the overview of omniscient authority.

It is true that, for a time, the large trading communities that had grown up in the Mediterranean were precariously protected against marauders by the still more martial Romans who, as Cicero tells us, could dominate the region by subduing the most advanced commercial centres of Corinth and Carthage, which had sacrificed military prowess to *mercandi et navigandi cupiditas* (*De re publica*, 2, 7–10). But during the last years of the Republic and the first centuries of the Empire, governed by a senate whose members were deeply involved in commercial interests, Rome gave the world the prototype of private law based on the most absolute conception of several property. The decline and final collapse of this first extended order came only after central administration in Rome increasingly displaced free endeavour. This sequence has been repeated again and again: civilisation might spread, but is not likely to advance much further, under a government that takes over the direction of daily affairs from its citizens. It would seem that no advanced civilisation has yet developed without a government which saw its chief aim in the protection of private property, but that again and again the further evolution and growth to which this gave rise was halted by a 'strong' government. Governments strong enough to protect individuals against the violence of their fellows make possible the evolution of an increasingly complex order of spontaneous and voluntary cooperation. Sooner or later, however, they tend to abuse that power and to suppress the freedom they had earlier secured in order to enforce their own presumedly greater wisdom and not to allow 'social institutions to develop in a haphazard manner' (to take a characteristic expression that is found under the heading 'social engineering' in the *Fontana/Harper Dictionary of Modern Thought* (1977)).

If the Roman decline did not permanently terminate the processes of evolution even in Europe, similar beginnings in Asia (and later independently in Meso-America) were stopped by powerful governments which (similar to but exceeding in power mediaeval feudal systems in Europe) also effectively suppressed private initiative. In the most remarkable of these, imperial China, great advances towards civilisation and towards sophisticated industrial technology took place

32

during recurrent 'times of trouble' when government control was temporarily weakened. But these rebellions or aberrances were regularly smothered by the might of a state preoccupied with the literal preservation of traditional order (J. Needham, 1954).

> This is also well illustrated in Egypt, where we have quite good information about the role that private property played in the initial rise of this great civilisation. In his study of Egyptian institutions and private law, Jacques Pirenne describes the essentially individualistic character of the law at the end of the third dynasty, when property was 'individual and inviolable, depending wholly on the proprietor' (Pirenne, 1934:II, 338–9), but records the beginning of its decay already during the fifth dynasty. This led to the state socialism of the eighteenth dynasty described in another French work of the same date (Dairaines, 1934), which prevailed for the next two thousand years and largely explains the stagnant character of Egyptian civilisation during that period.

Similarly, of the revival of European civilisation during the later Middle Ages it could be said that the expansion of capitalism – and European civilisation – owes its origins and *raison d'être* to political anarchy (Baechler, 1975:77). It was not under the more powerful governments, but in the towns of the Italian Renaissance, of South Germany and of the Low Countries, and finally in lightly-governed England, i.e., under the rule of the bourgeoisie rather than of warriors, that modern industrialism grew. Protection of several property, not the direction of its use by government, laid the foundations for the growth of the dense network of exchange of services that shaped the extended order.

Nothing is more misleading, then, than the conventional formulae of historians who represent the achievement of a powerful state as the culmination of cultural evolution: it as often marked its end. In this respect students of early history were overly impressed and greatly misled by monuments and documents left by the holders of political power, whereas the true builders of the extended order, who as often as not created the wealth that made the monuments possible, left less tangible and ostentatious testimonies to their achievement.

'Where There Is No Property There Is No Justice'

Nor did wise observers of the emerging extended order much doubt that it was rooted in the security, guaranteed by governments, that limited coercion to the enforcement of abstract rules determining what was to belong to whom. The 'possessive individualism' of John Locke was, for example, not just a political theory but the product of an analysis of the conditions to which England and Holland owed their prosperity. It was based in the insight that the *justice* that political authority must enforce, if it wants to secure the peaceful cooperation among individuals on which prosperity rests, cannot exist without the recognition of private property: ' "Where there is no property there is no justice," is a proposition as certain as any demonstration in Euclid: for the idea of property being a right to anything, and the idea to which the name of injustice is given being the invasion or violation of that right; it is evident that these ideas being thus established, and these names annexed to them, I can as certainly know this proposition to be true as that a triangle has three angles equal to two right ones' (John Locke: 1690/1924:IV, iii, 18). Soon afterwards, Montesquieu made known his message that it had been commerce that spread civilisation and sweet manners among the barbarians of Northern Europe.

For David Hume and other Scottish moralists and theorists of the eighteenth century, it was evident that the adoption of several property marks the beginning of civilisation; rules regulating property seemed so central to all morals that Hume devoted most of his *Treatise* on morals to them. It was to restrictions on government power to interfere with property that he later, in his *History of England* (Vol. V), ascribed that country's greatness; and in the *Treatise* itself (III, ii) he clearly explained that if mankind were to execute a law which, rather than establishing general rules governing ownership and exchange of property, instead 'assigned the largest possession to the most extensive virtue, . . . so great is the uncertainty of merit, both from the natural obscurity, and from the self-conceit of every individual, that no determinate rule of conduct would ever follow from it, and the total dissolution of society must be the immediate consequence'. Later, in the *Enquiry*, he remarked: 'Fanatics may suppose, that *domination is founded on grace, and that saints alone inherit the earth*; but the civil magistrate very justly puts these sublime theorists on the same footing with the common robbers, and teaches them by severe discipline, that a rule, which, in speculation, may seem the most advantageous to society, may yet be found, in practice, totally pernicious and destructive' (1777/1886:IV, 187).

Hume noticed clearly the connection of these doctrines to freedom, and how the maximum freedom of all requires equal restraints on the freedom of each through what he called the three 'fundamental laws of nature': 'the stability of possession, of its transference by consent, and of the performance of promises' (1739/1886:II, 288, 293). Though his views evidently derived in part from those of theorists of the common law, such as Sir Matthew Hale (1609–76), Hume may have been the first clearly to perceive that general freedom becomes possible by the natural moral instincts being 'checked and restrained by a subsequent judgement' according to '*justice*, or a regard to the property of others, *fidelity*, or the observance of promises [which have] become obligatory, and acquire[d] an authority over mankind' (1741, 1742/1886:III, 455). Hume did not make the error, later so common, of confusing two senses of freedom: that curious sense in which an isolated individual is supposed to be able to be free, and that in which many persons collaborating with one another can be free. Seen in the latter context of such collaboration, only abstract rules of property – i.e., the rules of law – guarantee freedom.

When Adam Ferguson summed up such teaching by defining the savage as a man who did not yet know property (1767/73:136), and when Adam Smith remarked that 'nobody ever saw one animal by its gestures or natural cries signify to another, this is mine, that is yours' (1776/1976:26), they expressed what, in spite of recurrent revolts by rapacious or hungry bands, had for practically two millennia been the view of the educated. As Ferguson put it, 'It must appear very evident, that property is a matter of progress' (ibid.). Such matters were, as we have noticed, also then investigated in language and the law; they were well understood in the classical liberalism of the nineteenth century; and it was probably through Edmund Burke, but perhaps even more through the influence of German linguists and lawyers like F. C. von Savigny, that these themes were then taken up again by H. S. Maine. Savigny's statement (in his protest against the codification of the civil law) deserves to be reproduced at length: 'If in such contacts free agents are to exist side by side, mutually supporting and not impeding each other in their development, this can be achieved only by recognising an invisible boundary within which the existence and operation of each individual is assured a certain free space. The rules by which these boundaries and through it the free range of each is determined is the law' (Savigny, 1840:I, 331–2).

The Various Forms and Objects of Property and the Improvement Thereof

The institutions of property, as they exist at present, are hardly perfect; indeed, we can hardly yet say in what such perfection might consist. Cultural and moral evolution do require further steps if the institution of several property is in fact to be as beneficial as it can be. For example, we need the general practice of competition to prevent abuse of property. This in turn requires further restraint on the innate feelings of the micro-order, the small group discussed earlier (see chapter one above, and Schoeck, 1966/69), for these instinctual feelings are often threatened not only by several property but sometimes even more so by competition, and this leads people to long doubly for non-competitive 'solidarity'.

While property is initially a product of custom, and jurisdiction and legislation have merely developed it in the course of millennia, there is then no reason to suppose that the particular forms it has assumed in the contemporary world are final. Traditional concepts of property rights have in recent times been recognised as a modifiable and very complex bundle whose most effective combinations have not yet been discovered in all areas. New investigations of these matters, originating largely in the stimulating but unfortunately uncompleted work of the late Sir Arnold Plant, have been taken up in a few brief but most influential essays by his former student Ronald Coase (1937 and 1960) which have stimulated the growth of an extensive 'property rights school' (Alchian, Becker, Cheung, Demsetz, Pejovich). The results of these investigations, which we cannot attempt to summarise here, have opened new possibilities for future improvements in the legal framework of the market order.

Just to illustrate how great our ignorance of the optimum forms of delimitation of various rights remains – despite our confidence in the indispensability of the general institution of several property – a few remarks about one particular form of property may be made.

The slow selection by trial and error of a system of rules delimiting individual ranges of control over different resources has created a curious position. Those very intellectuals who are generally inclined to question those forms of material property which are indispensable for the efficient organisation of the material means of production have become the most enthusiastic supporters of certain immaterial property rights invented only relatively recently, having to do, for example, with literary productions and technological inventions (i.e., copyrights and patents).

The difference between these and other kinds of property rights is this: while ownership of material goods guides the use of scarce means to their most important uses, in the case of immaterial goods such as literary productions and technological inventions the ability to produce them is also limited, yet once they have come into existence, they can be indefinitely multiplied and can be made scarce only by law in order to create an inducement to produce such ideas. Yet it is not obvious that such forced scarcity is the most effective way to stimulate the human creative process. I doubt whether there exists a single great work of literature which we would not possess had the author been unable to obtain an exclusive copyright for it; it seems to me that the case for copyright must rest almost entirely on the circumstance that such exceedingly useful works as encyclopaedias, dictionaries, textbooks and other works of reference could not be produced if, once they existed, they could freely be reproduced.

Similarly, recurrent re-examinations of the problem have not demonstrated that the obtainability of patents of invention actually enhances the flow of new technical knowledge rather than leading to wasteful concentration of research on problems whose solution in the near future can be foreseen and where, in consequence of the law, anyone who hits upon a solution a moment before the next gains the right to its exclusive use for a prolonged period (Machlup, 1962).

Organisations as Elements of Spontaneous Orders

Having written of the pretence of reason and the dangers of 'rational' interference with spontaneous order, I need to add yet another word of caution. My central aim has made it necessary to stress the spontaneous evolution of rules of conduct that assist the formation of self-organising structures. This emphasis on the spontaneous nature of the extended or macro-order could mislead if it conveyed the impression that, in the macro-order, deliberate organisation is never important.

The elements of the spontaneous macro-order are the several economic arrangements of individuals *as well as* those of deliberate organisations. Indeed, the evolution of individualist law consists in great measure in making possible the existence of voluntary associations without compulsory powers. But as the overall spontaneous order expands, so the sizes of the units of which it consists grow. Increasingly, its elements will not be economies of individuals, but of such organisations as firms and associations, as well as of administrative bodies. Among the rules of conduct that make it possible for extensive spontaneous orders to be formed, some will also facilitate deliberate organisations suited to operate within the larger systems. However, many of these various types of more comprehensive deliberate organisation actually have a place only within an even more comprehensive spontaneous order, and would be inappropriate within an overall order that was itself deliberately organised.

Another, related, matter could also mislead. Earlier we mentioned the growing differentiation of various kinds of property rights in a vertical or hierarchical dimension. If, elsewhere in this book, we occasionally speak about the rules of several property as if the contents of individual property were uniform and constant, this should be seen as a simplification that could mislead if understood without the qualifications already stated. This is in fact a field in which the greatest advances in the governmental framework of the spontaneous order may be expected, but which we cannot consider further here.

THE EVOLUTION OF THE MARKET:
TRADE AND CIVILISATION

What is worth Anything
But as Much Money as it Will Bring?

Samuel Butler

Ou il y a du commerce
Il y a des moeurs douces.

Montesquieu

The Expansion of Order into the Unknown

Having reviewed some of the circumstances in which the extended order arose, and how this order both engenders and requires several property, liberty and justice, we may now trace some further connections by looking more closely at some other matters already alluded to – in particular, the development of trade, and the specialisation that is linked to it. These developments, which also contributed greatly to the growth of an extended order, were little understood at the time, or indeed for centuries afterwards, even by the greatest scientists and philosophers; certainly no one ever deliberately arranged them.

The times, circumstances, and processes of which we write are cloaked in the mists of time, and details cannot be discerned with any confidence of accuracy. Some specialisation and exchange may already have developed in early small communities guided entirely by the consent of their members. Some nominal trade may have taken place as primitive men, following the migration of animals, encountered other men and groups of men. While archaeological evidence for very early trade is convincing it is not only rare but also tends to be misleading. The essentials that trade served to procure were mostly consumed without leaving a trace – whereas rarities brought to tempt their owners to part with these necessities were often meant to be kept and therefore more durable. Ornaments, weapons, and tools provide our chief positive evidence, while we can only infer from the absence in the locality of essential natural resources used in their manufacture that these must have been acquired by trade. Nor is archaeology likely to find the salt that people obtained over long distances; but the remuneration that the producers of salt received for selling it sometimes does remain. Yet it was not the desire for luxury but necessity that made trade an indispensable institution to which ancient communities increasingly owed their very existence.

However these things may be, trade certainly came very early, and trade over great distances, and in articles whose source is unlikely to have been known to those traders engaged in it, is far older than any other contact among remote groups that can now be traced. Modern archaeology confirms that trade is older than agriculture or any other sort of regular production (Leakey, 1981:212). In Europe there is evidence of trade over very great distances even in the Palaeolithic age, at least 30,000 years ago (Herskovits, 1948, 1960). Eight thousand years ago, Catal Hüyük in Anatolia and Jericho in Palestine had become centres of trade between the Black and the Red Seas, even before trade in pottery and metals had begun. Both also provide early instances of those 'dramatic increases of population' often described as cultural revolutions. Later, 'a network of shipping and land routes existed by the late seventh millennium B.C. for carrying obsidian from the island of Melos to the mainland' of Asia Minor and Greece (see S. Green's introduction to Childe, 1936/1981; and Renfrew, 1973:29, cf. also Renfrew, 1972:297–307). There is 'evidence for extensive trade networks linking Baluchistan (in West Pakistan) with regions in western Asia even before 3200 B.C.' (Childe, 1936/1981:19). We also know that the economy of predynastic Egypt was firmly based on trade (Pirenne, 1934).

The importance of regular trade in Homeric times is indicated by the story in the *Odyssey* (I, 180–184) in which Athena appears to Telemachos in the guise of the master of a ship carrying a cargo of iron to be exchanged for copper. The great expansion of trade which made possible the later rapid growth of classical civilisation appears from archaeological evidence also to have occurred at a time for which almost no historical documentation is available, that is, during the two hundred years from about 750 to 550 B.C. The expansion of trade also seems to have brought about, at roughly the same time, rapid increases of population in Greek and Phoenician centres of trade. These centres so rivalled each other in establishing colonies that by the beginning of the classical era life at the great centres of culture had become wholly dependent on a regular market process.

The existence of trade in these early times is incontestable, as is its role in spreading order. Yet the establishment of such a market process could hardly have been easy, and must have been accompanied by a substantial disruption of the early tribes. Even where some recognition of several property had emerged, further and previously unheard of practices would have been required before communities would be inclined to permit members to carry away for use by strangers (and for purposes only partly understood even by the traders themselves, let alone the local populace) desirable items held within the community that might otherwise have been available for local common use. For example, the shippers of the rising Greek cities who took pottery jugs filled with oil or wine to the Black Sea, Egypt or Sicily to exchange them for grain, in the process took away, to people of whom their neighbours knew virtually nothing, goods which those neighbours themselves much desired. By allowing this to happen, members of the small group must have lost their very bearings and begun to reorient to a new comprehension of the world, one in which the importance of the small group itself was much reduced. As Piggott explains in *Ancient Europe*, 'Prospectors and miners, traders and middlemen, the organis-ation of shipments and caravans, concessions and treaties, the concept of alien peoples and customs in distant lands – all these are involved in the enlargement of social comprehension demanded by the techno-logical step of entering . . . a bronze age' (Piggott, 1965:72). As the same author writes about the middle bronze age of the second millennium, 'The network of routes by sea, river and land gives an international character to much of the bronze-working of that time, and we find techniques and styles widely distributed from one end of Europe to the other' (ibid., 118).

What practices eased these new departures and ushered in not only a new comprehension of the world but even a kind of 'internationalisation' (the word is of course anachronistic) of style, technique, and attitudes? They must at least have included hospitality, protection, and safe passage (see next section). The vaguely defined territories of primitive tribes were presumably, even at an early date, interlaced by trading connections among individuals based on such practices. Such personal connections would provide successive links in chains over which small yet indispensable amounts of 'trace elements', as it were, were transmitted over great distances. This made sedentary occupations, and thus specialisation, possible in many new localities – and likewise eventually increased the density of population. A chain reaction began: the greater density of population, leading to the discovery of opportunities for specialisation, or division of labour, led to yet further increases of population and per capita income that made possible another increase in the population. And so on.

The Density of Occupation of the World Made Possible by Trade

This 'chain reaction' sparked by new settlement and trade may be studied more closely. While some animals are adapted to particular and rather limited environmental 'niches' outside of which they can hardly exist, men and a few other animals such as rats have been able to adapt themselves almost everywhere on the surface of the earth. This is hardly due merely to adaptations by *individuals*. Only a few and relatively small localities would have provided small bands of hunters and gatherers all that even the most primitive tool-using groups need for a settled existence, and still less all they needed to till the earth. Without support from fellows elsewhere, most humans would find the places they wish to occupy either uninhabitable or able to be settled only very thinly.

Those few relatively self-sustaining niches that did exist would likely be the first in any particular area to be permanently occupied and defended against intruders. Yet people living there would come to know of neighbouring places that provided most but not all their needs, and which would lack some substance they would require only occasionally: flint, strings for their bows, glues to fix cutting blades into handles, tanning materials for hides, and such like. Confident that such needs could be met by infrequent return visits to their present homes, they would stride out from their groups, and occupy some of these neighbouring places, or other new territory even further away in other parts of the thinly populated continents on which they lived. The importance of these early movements of persons and of necessary goods cannot be gauged by volume alone. Without the availability of imports, even if they formed only an insignificant fraction of what was currently being consumed in any particular place, it would have been impossible for early settlers to maintain themselves, let alone to multiply.

Return visits to replenish supplies would raise no difficulties so long as the migrants were still known to those who had remained at home. Within a few generations, however, descendants of these original groups would begin to seem strangers to one another; and those inhabiting the original more self-sustaining localities would often begin to defend themselves and their supplies in various ways. To gain permission to enter the original territory for the purpose of obtaining whatever special substances could be obtained only there, visitors would, to herald their peaceful intentions and to tempt the desires of its occupants, have had to bring presents. To be most effective, these gifts had best not satisfy everyday needs readily met locally, but would need to be enticingly new and unusual ornaments or delicacies. This is one reason why objects offered on one side of such transactions were, in fact, so often 'luxuries'

41

- which hardly means that the objects exchanged were not necessities for the other side.

Initially, regular connections involving exchange of presents would probably have developed between families with mutual obligations of hospitality connected in complex ways with the rituals of exogamy. The transition from the practice of giving presents to such family members and relations, to the appearance of more impersonal institutions of hosts or 'brokers' who routinely sponsored such visitors and gained for them permission to stay long enough to obtain what they needed, and on to the practice of exchanging particular things at rates determined by their relative scarcity, was no doubt slow. But from the recognition of a minimum still regarded as appropriate, and of a maximum at which the transaction seemed no longer worthwhile, specific prices for particular objects will gradually have emerged. Also inevitably, traditional equivalents will steadily have adapted to changed conditions.

In any case, in early Greek history we do find the important institution of the *xenos*, the guest-friend, who assured individual admission and protection within an alien territory. Indeed, trade must have developed very much as a matter of personal relations, even if the warrior aristocracy disguised it as being no more than mutual exchange of gifts. And it was not only those who were already wealthy who could afford hospitality to members of particular families in other regions: such relations also would have made people rich by providing channels through which important needs of their community could be satisfied. The *xenos* at Pylos and Sparta to whom Telemachos goes to get news of his 'much travelled father Odysseus' (*Odyssey*: III) was probably such a trading partner who by his wealth had risen to become king.

Such enlarged opportunities to deal advantageously with outsiders no doubt also helped to reinforce the break that had by then already occurred away from the solidarity, common aims, and collectivism of the original small groups. In any case, some individuals did tear away, or were released, from the hold and obligations of the small community, and began not only to settle other communities, but also to lay the foundations for a network of connections with members of still other communities – a network that ultimately, in countless relays and ramifications, has covered the whole earth. Such individuals were enabled to contribute their shares, albeit unknowingly and unintention- ally, towards the building of a more complex and extensive order – an order far beyond their own or their contemporaries' purview.

To create such an order, such individuals had to be able to use information for purposes known only to themselves. They could not have done so without the benefit of certain practices, such as that of the *xenos*, shared in common with distant groups. The practices would have to be common; but the particular knowledge and ends of those individuals following such practices could differ, and could be based on privileged information. This, in turn, would have spurred individual initiative.

For only an individual, not his group, could gain peaceful admission to an alien territory, and thereby acquire knowledge not possessed by his fellows. Trade could not be based on collective knowledge, only on distinctive individual knowledge. Only the growing recognition of several property could have made such use of individual initiative possible. The shippers and other traders were guided by personal gain; yet soon the wealth and livelihood of the growing population of their home towns, which they made possible through the pursuit of gain through trade rather than production, could be maintained only by their continuing initiative in discovering ever new opportunities.

Lest what we have just written mislead, it must be remembered that *why* men should ever have adopted any particular new custom or innovation is of secondary importance. What is more important is that in order for a custom or innovation to be preserved, there were two distinct prerequisites. Firstly, there must have existed some conditions that made possible the preservation through generations of certain practices whose benefits were not necessarily understood or appreciated. Secondly, there must have been the acquisition of distinct advantages by those groups that kept to such customs, thereby enabling them to expand more rapidly than others and ultimately to supersede (or absorb) those not possessing similar customs.

Trade Older than the State

That the human race eventually was able to occupy most of the earth as densely as it has done, enabling it to maintain large numbers even in regions where hardly any necessities of life can be produced locally, is the result of mankind's having learnt, like a single colossal body stretching itself, to extend to the remotest corners and pluck from each area different ingredients needed to nourish the whole. Indeed, it will perhaps not be long before even Antarctica will enable thousands of miners to earn an ample livelihood. To an observer from space, this covering of the earth's surface, with the increasingly changing appearance that it wrought, might seem like an organic growth. But it was no such thing: it was accomplished by individuals following not instinctual demands but traditional customs and rules.

These individual traders and hosts rarely know (as their predecessors rarely knew) all that much about the particular individual needs they serve. Nor do they need such knowledge. Many of these needs will indeed not even arise until a time so far in the future that nobody can foresee even its general outlines.

The more one learns about economic history, the more misleading then seems the belief that the achievement of a highly organised state constituted the culmination of the early development of civilisation. The role played by governments is greatly exaggerated in historical accounts because we necessarily know so much more about what organised government did than about what the spontaneous coordination of individual efforts accomplished. This deception, which stems from the nature of those things preserved, such as documents and monuments, is exemplified by the story (which I hope is apocryphal) about the archaeologist who concluded from the fact that the earliest reports of particular prices were inscribed on a stone pillar that prices had always been set by governments. Yet this is hardly worse than finding, in a well-known work, the argument that, since no suitable open spaces were found in the excavation of Babylonian cities, no regular markets could as yet have existed there – as if in a hot climate such markets would have been held in the open!

Governments have more often hindered than initiated the development of long-distance trade. Those that gave greater independence and security to individuals engaged in trading benefited from the increased information and larger population that resulted. Yet, when governments became aware how dependent their people had become on the importation of certain essential foodstuffs and materials, they themselves often endeavoured to secure these supplies in one way or another. Some early governments, for instance, after first learning from individual trade of the very existence of desirable resources, tried to obtain these resources by organising military or colonising expeditions. The Athenians were not the first and certainly not the last to attempt to do so. But it is absurd to conclude from this, as some modern writers have done (Polanyi, 1945, 1977), that, at the time of Athens's greatest prosperity and growth, its trade was 'administered', regulated by government through treaties and conducted at fixed prices.

Rather, it would seem as if, over and over again, powerful governments so badly damaged spontaneous improvement that the process of cultural evolution was brought to an early demise. The Byzantine government of the East Roman Empire may be one instance of this (Rostovtzeff, 1930, and Einaudi, 1948). And the history of China provides many instances of government attempts to enforce so perfect an order that innovation became impossible (Needham, 1954). This country, technologically and scientifically developed so far ahead of Europe that, to give only one illustration, it had ten oil wells operating on one stretch of the river Po already in the twelfth century, certainly owed its later stagnation, but not its early progress, to the manipulatory power of its governments. What led the greatly advanced civilisation of China to fall behind Europe was its governments' clamping down so tightly as to leave no room for new developments, while, as remarked in the last chapter, Europe probably owes its extraordinary expansion in the Middle Ages to its political anarchy (Baechler, 1975:77).

The Philosopher's Blindness

How little the wealth of the leading Greek trading centers, especially at Athens and later at Corinth, was the result of deliberate governmental policy, and how little the true source of this prosperity was understood, is perhaps best illustrated by Aristotle's utter incomprehension of the advanced market order in which he lived. Although he is sometimes cited as the first economist, what he discussed as *oikonomia* was exclusively the running of a household or at most of an individual enterprise such as a farm. For the acquisitive efforts of the market, the study of which he called *chrematistika*, he had only scorn. Although the lives of the Athenians of his day depended on grain trade with distant countries, his ideal order remained one that was *autarkos*, self-sufficient. Although also acclaimed as a biologist, Aristotle lacked any perception of two crucial aspects of the formation of any complex structure, namely, evolution and the self-formation of order. As Ernst Mayr (1982:306) puts it: 'The idea that the universe could have developed from an original chaos, or that higher organisms could have evolved from lower ones, was totally alien to Aristotle's thought. To repeat, Aristotle was opposed to evolution of any kind.' He seems not to have noticed the sense of 'nature' (or *physis*) as describing the process of growth (see Appendix A), and also seems to have been unfamiliar with several distinctions among self-forming orders that had been known to the pre-Socratic philosophers, such as that between a spontaneously grown *kosmos* and a deliberately arranged order as that of an army, which earlier thinkers had called a *taxis* (Hayek, 1973:37). For Aristotle, all order of human activities was *taxis*, the result of deliberate organisation of individual action by an ordering mind. As we saw earlier (chapter one), he expressly stated that order could be achieved only in a place small enough for everyone to hear the herald's cry, a place which could be easily surveyed (*eusynoptos*, *Politeia*: 1326b and 1327a). 'An excessively large number', he declared (1326a), 'cannot participate in order'.

To Aristotle, only the known needs of an existing population provided a natural or legitimate justification for economic effort. Mankind, and even nature, he treated as if they had always existed in their present

45

form. This static view left no room for a conception of evolution, and prevented him from even asking how existing institutions had arisen. That most existing communities, and certainly the greater number of his fellow Athenians, could not have come into existence had their forefathers remained content to satisfy their known present needs, appears never to have occurred to him. The experimental process of adaptation to unforeseen change by the observation of abstract rules which, when successful, could lead to an increase of numbers and the formation of regular patterns, was alien to him. Thus Aristotle also set the pattern for a common approach to ethical theory, one under which clues to the usefulness of rules that are offered by history go unrecognised, one under which no thought of analysing usefulness from an economic standpoint ever occurs – since the theorist is oblivious to the problems whose solutions might be embodied in such rules.

Since only actions aiming at *perceived benefit to others* were, to Aristotle's mind, morally approved, actions solely for personal gain must be bad. That commercial considerations may not have affected the daily activities of most people does not mean however that over any prolonged period their very lives did not depend on the functioning of a trade that enabled them to buy essentials. That production for gain which Aristotle denounced as unnatural had – long before his time – already become the foundation of an extended order far transcending the known needs of other persons.

As we now know, in the evolution of the structure of human activities, profitability works as a signal that guides selection towards what makes man more fruitful; only what is more profitable will, as a rule, nourish more people, for it sacrifices less than it adds. So much was at least sensed by some Greeks prior to Aristotle. Indeed, in the fifth century – that is, before Aristotle – the first truly great historian began his history of the Peloponnesian War by reflecting how early people 'without commerce, without freedom of communication either by land or sea, cultivating no more of their territory than the exigencies of life required, could never rise above nomadic life' and consequently 'neither built large cities nor attained to any other form of greatness' (Thucydides, Crawly translation, I,1,2). But Aristotle ignored this insight.

Had the Athenians followed Aristotle's counsel – counsel blind both to economics and to evolution – their city would rapidly have shrunk into a village, for his view of human ordering led him to an ethics appropriate only to, if anywhere at all, a stationary state. Nonetheless his doctrines came to dominate philosophical and religious thinking for the next two thousand years – despite the fact that much of that same philosophical and religious thinking took place within a highly dynamic, rapidly extending, order.

The repercussions of Aristotle's systematisation of the morals of the micro-order were amplified with the adoption of Aristotelian teaching in the thirteenth century by Thomas Aquinas, which later led to the proclamation of Aristotelian ethics as virtually the official teaching of the Roman Catholic Church. The anti-commercial attitude of the mediaeval and early modern Church, condemnation of interest as usury, its teaching of the just price, and its contemptuous treatment of gain is Aristotelian through and through.

By the eighteenth century, of course, Aristotle's influence in such matters (as in others) was weakening. David Hume saw that the market made it possible 'to do a service to another without bearing him a real kindness' (1739/1886:II, 289) or even knowing him; or to act to the 'advantage of the public, though it be not intended for that purpose by another' (1739/1886:II, 296), by an order in which it was in the 'interest, even of bad men to act for the public good'. With such insights, the conception of a self-organising structure began to dawn upon mankind, and has since become the basis of our understanding of all those complex orders which had, until then, appeared as miracles that could be brought about only by some super-human version of what man knew as his own mind. Now it gradually became understood how the market enabled each, within set limits, to use his own individual knowledge for his own individual purposes while being ignorant of most of the order into which he had to fit his actions.

Notwithstanding, and indeed wholly neglecting, the existence of this great advance, a view that is still permeated by Aristotelian thought, a naive and childlike animistic view of the world (Piaget, 1929:359), has come to dominate social theory and is the foundation of socialist thought.

FOUR

THE REVOLT OF INSTINCT AND REASON

It is necessary to guard ourselves from thinking that the practice of the scientific method enlarges the powers of the human mind. Nothing is more flatly contradicted by experience than the belief that a man distinguished in one or even more departments of science, is more likely to think sensibly about ordinary affairs than anyone else.

Wilfred Trotter

The Challenge to Property

Although Aristotle was blind to the importance of trade, and lacked any comprehension of evolution; and though Aristotelian thought, once embedded in the system of Thomas Aquinas, supported the anti-commercial attitudes of the mediaeval and early modern Church, it was nonetheless only rather later, and chiefly among seventeenth- and eighteenth-century French thinkers, that several important developments occurred which, taken together, began effectively to challenge the central values and institutions of the extended order.

The first of these developments was the growing importance, associated with the rise of modern science, of that particular form of rationalism that I call 'constructivism' or 'scientism' (after the French), which for the following several centuries virtually captured serious thought about reason and its role in human affairs. This particular form of rationalism has been the point of departure of investigations that I have conducted over the past sixty years, investigations in which I tried to show that it is particularly ill-considered, embedding a false theory of science and of rationality in which reason is *abused*, and which, most important here, leads invariably to an erroneous interpretation of the nature and coming into being of human institutions. That interpretation is one by which, in the *name* of reason and the highest values of civilisation, moralists end up flattering the relatively unsuccessful and inciting people to satisfy their primitive desires.

Descending in the modern period from René Descartes, this form of rationalism not only discards tradition, but claims that pure reason can directly serve our desires without any such intermediary, and can build a new world, a new morality, a new law, even a new and purified language, from itself alone. Although the theory is plainly false (see also Popper, 1934/1959, and 1945/66), it still dominates the thinking of most scientists, and also of most literati, artists, and intellectuals.

I should perhaps immediately qualify what I have just written by adding that there are other strands within what might be called rationalism which treat these matters differently, as for example that which views rules of moral conduct as themselves *part* of reason. Thus John Locke had explained that 'by reason, however, I do not think is meant here the faculty of understanding which forms trains of thoughts and deduces proofs, but definite principles of action from which spring all virtues and whatever is necessary for the moulding of morals' (1954:11). Yet views such as Locke's remain much in the minority among those who call themselves rationalists.

The second, related development which challenged the extended order arose from the work and influence of Jean–Jacques Rousseau. This peculiar thinker – although often described as irrationalist or romantic – also latched on to and deeply depended on Cartesian thought. Rousseau's heady brew of ideas came to dominate 'progressive' thought, and led people to forget that freedom as a political institution had arisen *not* by human beings 'striving for freedom' in the sense of release from restraints, but by their striving for the protection of a known secure individual domain. Rousseau led people to forget that rules of conduct necessarily constrain and that order is their product; and that these rules, precisely by limiting the range of means that each individual may use for his purposes, greatly extend the range of ends each can successfully pursue.

It was Rousseau who – declaring in the opening statement of *The Social Contract* that 'man was born free, and he is everywhere in chains', and wanting to free men from all 'artificial' restraints – made what had been called the savage the virtual hero of progressive intellectuals, urged people to shake off the very restraints to which they owed their productivity and numbers, and produced a conception of liberty that became the greatest obstacle to its attainment. After asserting that animal instinct was a better guide to orderly cooperation among men than *either* tradition or reason, Rousseau invented the fictitious will of the people, or 'general will', through which the people 'becomes one single being, one individual' (*Social Contract*, I, vii; and see Popper, 1945/1966:II, 54). This is perhaps the chief source of the fatal conceit of modern intellectual rationalism that promises to lead us back to a paradise wherein our natural instincts rather than learnt restraints upon them will enable us 'to subdue the world', as we are instructed in the book of *Genesis*.

49

The admittedly great seductive appeal of this view hardly owes its power (whatever it may claim) to reason and evidence. As we have seen, the savage was far from free; nor could he have subdued the world. He could indeed do little unless the whole group to which he belonged agreed. Individual decision presupposed individual spheres of control, and thus became possible only with the evolution of several property, whose development, in turn, laid the foundation for the growth of an extended order transcending the perception of the headman or chief – or of the collectivity.

Despite these contradictions, there is no doubt that Rousseau's outcry was effective or that, during the past two centuries, it has shaken our civilisation. Moreover, irrationalist as it is, it nonetheless did appeal precisely to progressivists by its Cartesian insinuation that we might use *reason* to obtain and justify direct gratification of our natural instincts. After Rousseau gave intellectual license to throw off cultural restraints, to confer legitimacy on attempts to gain 'freedom' from the restraints that had made freedom possible, and to *call* this attack on the foundation of freedom 'liberation', property became increasingly suspect and was no longer so widely recognised as the key factor that had brought about the extended order. It was increasingly supposed, rather, that rules regulating the delimitation and transfer of several property might be replaced by central decision about its use.

Indeed, by the nineteenth century, serious intellectual appreciation and discussion of the role of property in the development of civilisation would seem to have fallen under a kind of ban in many quarters. During this time property gradually became suspect among many of those who might have been expected to investigate it, a topic to be avoided by progressive believers in a rational reshaping of the structure of human cooperation. (That this ban has persisted into the twentieth century is evinced by, for example, Brian Barry's declarations (1961:80) about usage and 'analyticity', wherein justice 'is now analytically tied to "desert" and "need", so that one could say quite properly that some of what Hume called "rules of justice" were unjust', and Gunnar Myrdal's later mocking remark about the 'taboos of property and contract' (1969:17).) The founders of anthropology, for instance, increasingly neglected the cultural role of property, so that in E. B. Tylor's two volumes on *Primitive Culture* (1871), for instance, neither property nor ownership appear in the index, while E. Westermarck – who did devote a long chapter to property – already treats it, under the influence of Saint–Simon and Marx, as the objectionable source of 'unearned income', and concludes from this that the 'law of property will sooner or later undergo a radical change' (1908:II, 71). The socialist bias of constructivism has also influenced contemporary archaeology, but it displays its inability to comprehend economic phenomena most crudely in sociology (and even worse in the so-called 'sociology of knowledge'). Sociology itself might almost be called a socialist science, having been openly presented as capable of creating a new order of socialism (Ferri, 1895), or more recently able 'to predict the future development and to shape the future, or . . . create the future of mankind' (Segerstedt, 1969:441). Like the 'naturology' that once pretended to replace all specialised investigations of nature, sociology proceeds in sovereign disregard of knowledge gained by established disciplines that have long studied such grown structures as law, language, and the market.

I have just written that the study of traditional institutions such as property 'fell under a ban'. This is hardly an exaggeration, for it is highly curious that so interesting and important a process as the evolutionary selection of moral traditions has been so little studied, and the direction these traditions gave to the development of civilisation so largely ignored. Of course this will not seem so peculiar to a constructivist. If one suffers under the delusion of 'social engineering', the notion that man can consciously choose where he wants to go, it will not seem so important to discover how he reached his present situation.

It may be mentioned in passing, although I cannot explore the matter here, that challenges to property and traditional values came not only from followers of Rousseau: they also stemmed, although perhaps less importantly, from religion. For the revolutionary movements of this period (rationalistic socialism and then communism) helped to revive old heretical traditions of religious revolt against basic institutions of property and family – revolts directed in earlier centuries by heretics such as the Gnostics, the Manichaeans, the Bogomils, and the Cathars. By the nineteenth century, these particular heretics were gone, but thousands of new religious revolutionaries appeared who directed much of their zeal against both property and the family, also appealing to primitive instincts against such restraints. Rebellion against private property and the family was, in short, not restricted to socialists. Mystic and supernatural beliefs were invoked not only to justify customary restraints upon instincts, as for example in the dominant streams of Roman Catholicism and Protestantism, but also, in more peripheral movements, to support the release of instincts.

Limits of space as well as insufficient competence forbid me to deal in this book with the second of the traditional objects of atavistic reaction that I have just mentioned: the family. I ought however at least to mention that I believe that new factual knowledge has in some measure deprived traditional rules of sexual morality of some of their foundation, and that it seems likely that in this area substantial changes are bound to occur.

51

Having mentioned Rousseau and his pervasive influence, as well as these other historical developments, if only to remind readers that the revolt against property and traditional morality on the part of serious thinkers is not just comparatively recent, I shall turn now to some twentieth-century intellectual heirs of Rousseau and Descartes.

First, however, I should emphasise that I am largely neglecting here the long history of this revolt, as well as the different turns it has taken in different lands. Long before Auguste Comte introduced the term 'positivism' for the view that represented a 'demonstrated ethics' (demonstrated by reason, that is) as the only possible alternative to a supernaturally 'revealed ethics' (1854:I, 356), Jeremy Bentham had developed the most consistent foundations of what we now call legal and moral positivism: that is, the constructivistic interpretation of systems of law and morals according to which their validity and meaning are supposed to depend wholly on the will and intention of their designers. Bentham is himself a late figure in this development. This constructivism includes not only the Benthamite tradition, represented and continued by John Stuart Mill and the later English Liberal Party, but also practically all contemporary Americans who call themselves 'liberals' (as opposed to some other very different thinkers, more often found in Europe, who are also called liberals, who are better called 'old Whigs', and whose outstanding thinkers were Alexis de Tocqueville and Lord Acton). This constructivist way of thinking becomes virtually inevitable if, as an acute contemporary Swiss analyst suggests, one accepts the prevailing liberal (read 'socialist') philosophy that assumes that man, so far as the distinction between good and bad has any significance for him at all, must, and can, himself deliberately draw the line between them (Kirsch, 1981:17).

Our Intellectuals and Their Tradition of Reasonable Socialism

What I have suggested about morals and tradition, about economics and the market, and about evolution, obviously conflicts with many influential ideas, not only with the old Social Darwinism discussed in the first chapter, which is no longer widely held, but also with many other viewpoints past and present: with the views of Plato and Aristotle, of Rousseau and the founders of socialism, with those of Saint–Simon, Karl Marx, and many others.

Indeed, the basic point of my argument – that morals, including, especially, our institutions of property, freedom and justice, are not a creation of man's reason but a distinct second endowment conferred on him by cultural evolution – runs counter to the main intellectual outlook of the twentieth century. The influence of rationalism has indeed been so profound and pervasive that, in general, the more intelligent an educated person is, the more likely he or she now is not only to be a rationalist, but also to hold socialist views (regardless of whether he or she is sufficiently doctrinal to attach to his or her views any label, including 'socialist'). The higher we climb up the ladder of intelligence, the more we talk with intellectuals, the more likely we are to encounter socialist convictions. Rationalists tend to be intelligent and intellectual; and intelligent intellectuals tend to be socialists.

If I may insert two personal remarks here, I suppose that I can claim to speak with some experience about this outlook because these rationalist views that I have been systematically examining and criticising now for so many years are those on which I, in common with most non-religious European thinkers of my generation, formed my own outlook in the early part of this century. At that time they appeared self-evident, and following them seemed the way to escape pernicious superstitions of all sorts. Having myself spent some time in struggling free from these notions – indeed, discovering in the process that they themselves are superstitions – I can hardly intend personally some of my rather harsh remarks about particular authors in the pages that follow.

Moreover, it is perhaps appropriate to remind readers in this place of my essay 'On Why I Am Not a Conservative' (1960: Postscript), lest they draw inaccurate conclusions. Although my argument is directed against socialism, I am as little a Tory-Conservative as was Edmund Burke. My conservatism, such as it is, is entirely confined to morals within certain limits. I am entirely in favour of experimentation – indeed for very much more freedom than conservative governments tend to allow. What I object to among rationalist intellectuals such as those I shall be discussing is not that they experiment; rather, they experiment all too little, and what they fancy to be experimentation turns out mostly to be banal – after all, the idea of returning to instinct is really as common as rain and has by now been tried out so often that it is no longer clear in what sense it can any longer be called experimental. I object to such rationalists because they declare their experiments, such as they are, to be the results of reason, dress them up in pseudo-scientific methodology, and thus, whilst wooing influential recruits and subjecting invaluable traditional practices (the result of ages of evolutionary trial-and-error experiment) to unfounded attack, shelter their own 'experiments' from scrutiny.

One's initial surprise at finding that intelligent people tend to be socialists diminishes when one realises that, of course, intelligent people will tend to overvalue intelligence, and to suppose that we must owe all the advantages and opportunities that our civilisation offers to deliberate design rather than to following traditional rules, and likewise to suppose that we can, by exercising our reason, eliminate any remaining undesired features by still more intelligent reflection, and still more appropriate design and 'rational coordination' of our undertakings. This leads one to be favourably disposed to the central economic planning and control that lie at the heart of socialism. Of course intellectuals will demand explanations for everything they are expected to do, and will be reluctant to accept practices just because they happen to govern the communities into which they happen to have been born; and this will lead them into conflict with, or at least to a low opinion of, those who quietly accept prevailing rules of conduct. Moreover, they also understandably will want to align themselves with science and reason, and with the extraordinary progress made by the physical sciences during the past several centuries, and since they have been taught that constructivism and scientism are what science and the use of reason are all about, they find it hard to believe that there can exist any useful knowledge that did not originate in deliberate experimentation, or to accept the validity of any tradition apart from their own tradition of reason. Thus a distinguished historian has written in this vein: 'Tradition is almost by definition reprehensible, something to be mocked and deplored' (Seton–Watson, 1983:1270).

> *By definition*: Barry (1961, mentioned above) wanted to make morality and justice immoral and unjust by 'analytic definition'; here Seton–Watson would try the same manoeuvre with tradition, making it by definition reprehensible. We shall return to these *words*, to this 'Newspeak', in chapter seven. Meanwhile let us look more closely at the facts.

These reactions are all understandable, but they have consequences. The consequences are particularly dangerous – to reason as well as to morality – when preference not so much for the real products of reason as for this conventional tradition of reason leads intellectuals to ignore the theoretical limits of reason, to disregard a world of historical and scientific information, to remain ignorant of the biological sciences and the sciences of man such as economics, and to misrepresent the origin and functions of our traditional moral rules.

Like other traditions, the tradition of reason is learnt, not innate. It too lies *between instinct and reason; and the question of the real reasonableness and truth of this tradition of proclaimed reason and truth must now also scrupulously be examined.*

Morals and Reason: Some Examples

Lest I be thought to exaggerate, I shall provide, in a moment, a few examples. But I do not want to be unfair to our great scientists and philosophers, some of whose ideas I shall discuss. Although they, in their own opinions, illustrate the significance of the problem – that our philosophy and natural science are far from understanding the role played by our chief traditions – they themselves are not usually directly responsible for the wide dissemination of these ideas, for they have better things to do. On the other hand, it should also not be supposed that the remarks I am about to cite are merely momentary or idiosyncratic aberrations on the part of their distinguished authors: rather, they are consistent conclusions drawn from a well-established rationalist tradition. And indeed I do not doubt that some of these great thinkers have striven to comprehend the extended order of human cooperation – if only to end as determined, and often unwitting, opponents of this order.

Those who have really done most to spread these ideas, the real bearers of constructivist rationalism and socialism, are, however, not these distinguished scientists. They rather tend to be the so-called 'intellectuals' that I have elsewhere (1949/1967:178–94) unkindly called professional 'second-hand dealers in ideas': teachers, journalists and 'media representatives' who, having absorbed rumours in the corridors of science, appoint themselves as representatives of modern thought, as persons superior in knowledge and moral virtue to any who retain a high regard for traditional values, as persons whose very duty it is to offer new ideas to the public – and who must, in order to make their wares seem novel, deride whatever is conventional. For such people, due to the positions in which they find themselves, 'newness', or 'news', and not truth, becomes the main value, although that is hardly their intention – and although what they offer is often no more new than it is true. Moreover, one might wonder whether these intellectuals are not sometimes inspired by resentment that they, knowing better what ought to be done, are paid so much less than those whose instructions and activities in fact guide practical affairs. Such literary interpreters of scientific and technological advance, of which H. G. Wells, because of the unusually high quality of his work, would be an excellent example, have done far more to spread the socialist ideal of a centrally directed economy in which each is assigned his due share than have the real scientists from whom they have cadged many of their notions. Another such example is that of the early George Orwell, who once argued that 'anyone who uses his brain knows perfectly well that it is within the range of possibility [that] the world, potentially at least, is extremely rich' such that we could 'develop it as it might be developed, and we could all live like princes, supposing that we wanted to'.

I shall concentrate here not on the work of men like Wells and Orwell, but on views propounded by some of the greatest scientists. We might begin with Jacques Monod. Monod was a great figure whose scientific work I much admire, and was, essentially, the creator of modern molecular biology. His reflections on ethics, however, were of a different quality. In 1970, in a Nobel Foundation symposium concerning 'The Place of Values in a World of Facts', he stated: 'Scientific development has finally destroyed, reduced to absurdity, relegated to the state of nonsensical wishful thinking, the idea that ethics and values are not a matter of our free choice but are rather a matter of obligation for us' (1970:20–21). Later that year, to re-emphasise his views, he argued the same case in a book now famous, *Chance and Necessity* (1970/1977). There he enjoins us, ascetically renouncing all other spiritual nourishment, to acknowledge science as the new and virtually exclusive source of truth, and to revise the foundations of ethics accordingly. The book ends like so many similar pronouncements with the idea that 'ethics, in essence *nonobjective*, is forever barred from the sphere of knowledge' (1970/77:162). The new 'ethic of knowledge does not impose itself on man; *on the contrary, it is he who imposes it upon himself* (1970/77:164). This new 'ethic of knowledge' is, Monod says, 'the only attitude which is both rational and resolutely idealistic, and on which a real socialism might be built' (1970/77:165–66). Monod's ideas are characteristic in that they are deeply rooted in a theory of knowledge that has attempted to develop a science of behaviour – whether called eudaimonism, utilitarianism, socialism, or whatever – on the grounds that *certain sorts of behaviour better satisfy our wishes*. We are advised to behave in such a way as will permit given situations to satisfy our desires, and make us happier, and such like. In other words, what is wanted is an ethics that men can *deliberately* follow to reach *known*, desired, and pre-selected aims.

Monod's conclusions stem from his opinion that the only other possible way to account for the origin of morals – apart from ascribing them to human invention – is by animistic or anthropomorphic accounts such as are given in many religions. And it is indeed true that 'for mankind as a whole all religions have been intertwined with the anthropomorphic view of the deity as a father, friend or potentate to whom men must do service, pray, etc.' (M. R. Cohen, 1931:112). This aspect of religion I can as little accept as can Monod and the majority of natural scientists. It seems to me to lower something far beyond our comprehension to the level of a slightly superior manlike mind. But to reject this aspect of religion does not preclude our recognising that we may owe to these religions the preservation – admittedly for false reasons – of practices that were more important in enabling man to survive in large numbers than most of what has been accomplished through reason (see chapter nine below).

Monod is not the only biologist to argue along such lines. A statement by another great biologist and very learned scholar illustrates better than almost any other I have come across the absurdities to which supreme intelligence can be led by a misinterpretation of the 'laws of evolution' (see chapter one above). Joseph Needham writes that 'the new world order of social justice and comradeship, the rational and classless state, is no wild idealistic dream, but a logical extrapolation from the whole course of evolution, having no less authority than that behind it, and therefore of all faiths the most rational' (J. Needham, 1943:41).

I shall return to Monod, but want first to assemble a few further examples. A particularly appropriate instance that I have discussed elsewhere (1978), is John Maynard Keynes, one of the most representative intellectual leaders of a generation emancipated from traditional morals. Keynes believed that, by taking account of foreseeable effects, he could build a better world than by submitting to traditional abstract rules. Keynes used the phrase 'conventional wisdom' as a favourite expression of scorn, and, in a revealing autobiographical account (1938/49/72: X, 446), he told how the Cambridge circle of his younger years, most of whose members later belonged to the Bloomsbury Group, 'entirely repudiated a personal liability on us to obey general rules', and how they were 'in the strict sense of the term, immoralists'. He modestly added that, at the age of fifty-five, he was too old to change and would remain an immoralist. This extraordinary man also characteristically justified some of his economic views, and his general belief in a management of the market order, on the ground that 'in the long run we are all dead' (i.e., it does not matter what long-range damage we do; it is the present moment alone, the short run – consisting of public opinion, demands, votes, and all the stuff and bribes of demagoguery – which counts). The slogan that 'in the long run we are all dead' is also a characteristic manifestation of an unwillingness to recognise that morals are concerned with effects in the long run – effects *beyond our possible perception* – and of a tendency to spurn the learnt discipline of the long view.

Keynes also argued against the moral tradition of the 'virtue of saving', refusing, along with thousands of crank economists, to admit that a reduction of the demand for consumers' goods is generally required to make an increase of the production of capital goods (i.e., investment) possible.

And this in turn led him to devote his formidable intellectual powers to develop his 'general' theory of economics – to which we owe the unique world-wide inflation of the third quarter of our century and the inevitable consequence of severe unemployment that has followed it (Hayek, 1972/1978).

Thus it was not philosophy alone that confused Keynes. It was also economics. Alfred Marshall, who understood the matter, seems to have failed to impress adequately upon Keynes one of the important insights that John Stuart Mill had gained in his youth: namely, that 'the demand for commodities is not a demand for labour'. Sir Leslie Stephen (the father of Virginia Woolf, another member of the Bloomsbury group) described this doctrine in 1876 as a 'doctrine so rarely understood, that its complete appreciation is, perhaps, the best test of an economist' – and was ridiculed for saying so by Keynes. (See Hayek, 1970/78:15–16, 1973:25, and (on Mill and Stephen) 1941:433ff.)

Although Keynes was, in spite of himself, to contribute greatly to the weakening of freedom, he shocked his Bloomsbury friends by not sharing their general socialism; yet most of his students were socialists of one sort or other. Neither he nor these students recognised how the extended order must be based on long-run considerations.

The philosophic illusion that lay behind the views of Keynes, that there exists an indefinable attribute of 'goodness' – one to be discovered by every individual, which imposes on each a duty to pursue it, and whose recognition justifies contempt for and disregard of much of traditional morals (a view which through the work of G. E. Moore (1903) dominated the Bloomsbury group) – produced a characteristic enmity to the sources on which he fed. This was evident for instance also in E. M. Forster, who seriously argued that freeing mankind from the evils of 'commercialism' had become as urgent as had been freeing it from slavery.

Sentiments similar to those of Monod and Keynes come from a less distinguished yet still influential scientist: the psychoanalyst who became the first Secretary General of the World Health Organisation, G. B. Chisholm. Chisholm advocated no less than 'the eradication of the concept of right and wrong' and maintained that it was the task of the psychiatrist to free the human race from 'the crippling burden of good and evil' – advice which at the time received praise from high American legal authority. Here again, morality is seen – since it is not 'scientifically' grounded – as irrational, and its status as embodiment of accumulated cultural knowledge goes unrecognised.

Let us turn, however, to a scientist even greater than Monod or Keynes, to Albert Einstein, perhaps the greatest genius of our age.

Einstein was concerned with a different yet closely related theme. Using a popular socialist slogan, he wrote that 'production for use' ought to replace the 'production for profit' of the capitalist order (1956:129).

'Production for use' means here the kind of work which, in the small group, is guided by anticipating for whose use the product is intended. But this sentiment fails to take into account the sorts of considerations advanced in the foregoing chapters, and to be argued again in the following: only the differences between expected prices for different commodities and services and their costs, in the self-generating order of the market, tell the individual how best to contribute to the pool from which we all draw in proportion to our contribution. Einstein appears to have been unaware that only calculation and distribution in terms of market prices make it possible to utilise our discoverable resources intensively, to guide production to serve ends lying beyond the range of the producer's perception, and to enable the individual to participate usefully in productive exchange (first, by serving people, mostly unknown to him, to the gratification of whose needs he can nonetheless effectively contribute; and second, by himself being supplied as well as he is only because people who know nothing about *his* existence are induced, also by market signals, to provide for his needs: see the previous chapter). In following such sentiments Einstein shows his lack of comprehension of, or real interest in, the actual processes by which human efforts are coordinated.

Einstein's biographer reports that Einstein regarded it as obvious that 'human reason must be capable of finding a method of distribution which would work as effectively as that of production' (Clark, 1971:559) – a description that reminds one of the philosopher Bertrand Russell's claim that a society could not be regarded as 'fully scientific' unless 'it has been created deliberately with a certain structure to fulfil certain purposes' (1931:203). Such demands, particularly in Einstein's mouth, seemed so superficially plausible that even a sensible philosopher, twitting Einstein for talking beyond his competence in some of his popular writings, stated approvingly that 'Einstein is clearly aware that the present economic crisis is due to our system of production for profit rather than for use, to the fact that our tremendous increase of productive power is not actually followed by a corresponding increase in the purchasing power of the great masses' (M. R. Cohen, 1931:119).

We also find Einstein repeating (in the essay cited) familiar phrases of socialist agitation about the 'economic anarchy of capitalist society' in which 'the payment of the workers is not determined by the value of the product', while 'a planned economy . . . would distribute the work to be done among all those able to work', and such like.

A similar but more guarded view appears in an essay by Einstein's collaborator Max Born (1968: chap.5). While Born evidently realised that our extended order no longer gratified primitive instincts, he too failed to examine closely the structures that create and maintain this order, or to see that our instinctual morals have over the past five thousand years or more gradually been replaced or restrained. Thus, although perceiving that 'science and technology have destroyed the ethical basis of civilisation, perhaps irreparably', he imagines that they have done so by the facts they have uncovered rather than by their having systematically discredited beliefs that fail to satisfy certain 'standards of acceptability' demanded by constructivist rationalism (see below). While admitting that 'no one has yet devised a means of keeping society together without traditional ethical principles', Born yet hopes that these can be replaced 'by means of the traditional method used in science'. He too fails to see that what lies *between* instinct and reason cannot be replaced by 'the traditional method used in science'.

My examples are taken from statements of important twentieth-century figures; I have not included countless other such figures, such as R. A. Millikan, Arthur Eddington, F. Soddy, W. Ostwald, E. Solvay, J. D. Bernal, all of whom talked much nonsense on economic matters. Indeed, one could cite hundreds of similar statements by scientists and philosophers of comparable renown – both from centuries past and from the present time. But we can, I believe, learn more by taking a closer look at these particular contemporary examples – and at what lies behind them – than simply by piling up citations and examples. Perhaps the first thing to notice is that, although far from identical, these examples have a certain family resemblance.

A Litany of Errors

The ideas raised in these examples have in common a number of closely interconnected thematic roots, roots that are not just matters of common historical antecedents. Readers unfamiliar with some of the background literature may not immediately see some of the interconnections. Hence I should like, before further probing these ideas themselves, to identify a number of recurring themes – most of which may appear at first glance to be unobjectionable and all of which are familiar – which, taken together, form a sort of argument. This 'argument' could also be described as a litany of errors, or as a recipe for producing the presumptive rationalism that I call scientism and constructivism. To start on our way, let us consult that ready 'source of knowledge', the dictionary, a book containing many recipes. I have gathered from the very useful *Fontana/Harper Dictionary of Modern Thought* (1977) a few short definitions of four basic philosophical concepts that generally guide contemporary thinkers educated along scientistic and constructivistic lines: rationalism, empiricism, positivism, and utilitarianism – concepts which have, during the past several hundred years, come to be regarded as representative expressions of the scientific 'spirit of the age'. According to these definitions, which are written by Lord Quinton, a British philosopher who is President of Trinity College, Oxford, *rationalism* denies the acceptability of beliefs founded on anything but experience and reasoning, deductive or inductive. *Empiricism* maintains that all statements claiming to express knowledge are limited to those depending for their justification on experience. *Positivism* is defined as the view that all true knowledge is scientific, in the sense of describing the coexistence and succession of observable phenomena. And *utilitarianism* 'takes the pleasure and pain of everyone affected by it to be the criterion of the action's rightness'.

In such definitions one finds quite explicitly, just as one finds implicitly in the examples cited in the preceding section, the declarations of faith of modern science and philosophy of science, and their declarations of war against moral traditions. These declarations, definitions, postulates, have created the impression that only that which is rationally justifiable, only that which is provable by observational experiment, only that which can be experienced, only that which can be surveyed, deserves belief; that only that which is pleasurable should be acted upon, and that all else must be repudiated. This in turn leads directly to the contention that the leading moral traditions that have created and are creating our culture – which certainly cannot be justified in such ways, and which are often disliked – are unworthy of adherence, and that our task must be to construct a new morality on the basis of scientific knowledge – usually the new morality of socialism.

These definitions, together with our earlier examples, when examined more closely, prove indeed to contain the following presuppositions:

1) The idea that it is unreasonable to follow what one cannot justify scientifically or prove observationally (Monod, Born).

2) The idea that it is unreasonable to follow what one does not understand. This notion is implicit in all our examples, but I must confess that I too once held it, and have also been able to find it in a philosopher with whom I generally agree. Thus Sir Karl Popper once claimed (1948/63:122; emphasis added) that rationalist thinkers 'will not submit blindly to *any* tradition', which is of course just as impossible as obeying no tradition. This must, however, have been a slip of the pen, for elsewhere he has rightly observed that 'we never know what we are talking about' (1974/1976:27, on which see also Bartley, 1985/1987).

61

(Though the free man will insist on his right to examine and, when appropriate, to reject any tradition, he could not live among other people if he refused to accept countless traditions without even thinking about them, and of whose effects he remains ignorant.)

3) The related idea that it is unreasonable to follow a particular course unless its *purpose* is fully specified in advance (Einstein, Russell, Keynes).

4) The idea, also closely related, that it is unreasonable to do anything unless its *effects* are not only fully known in advance but also fully observable and seen to be beneficial (the utilitarians). (Assumptions 2, 3, and 4, are, despite their different emphases, nearly identical; but I have distinguished them here to call attention to the fact that the arguments for them turn, depending on who is defending them, either on lack of understandability generally, or, more particularly, on lack of specified purpose or lack of complete and observable knowledge of effects.)

One could name further requirements, but these four – which we shall examine in the following two chapters – will suffice for our (largely illustrative) purposes. Two things might be noticed about these requirements from the very start. First, not one of them shows any awareness that there might be limits to our knowledge or reason in certain areas, or considers that, in such circumstances, the most important task of science might be to discover what these limits are. We shall learn below that there are such limits and that they can indeed partially be overcome, as for example through the science of economics or 'catallactics', but that *they cannot be overcome if one holds to the above four requirements*. Second, one finds in the approach underlying the requirements not only lack of understanding, not only the failure to consider or deal with such problems, but also a curious lack of curiosity about how our extended order actually came into being, how it is maintained, and what the consequences might be of destroying those traditions that created and maintain it.

Positive and Negative Liberty

Some rationalists would want to advance an additional complaint that we have hardly considered: namely, that the morality and institutions of capitalism not only fail to meet the logical, methodological, and epistemological requirements reviewed already, but also impose a crippling burden on our freedom – as, for example, our freedom to 'express' ourselves unrestrainedly.

This complaint cannot be met by denying the obvious, a truth with which we opened this book – that moral tradition does seem burdensome to many – but can only be answered by observing again, here and in subsequent chapters, what we derive from bearing this burden, and what the alternative would be. Virtually all the benefits of civilisation, and indeed our very existence, rest, I believe, on our continuing willingness to shoulder the burden of tradition. These benefits in no way 'justify' the burden. But the alternative is poverty and famine.

Without attempting to recount or review all these benefits, to 'count our blessings', as it were, I may mention again, in a somewhat different context, perhaps the most ironic benefit of all – for I have in mind our very freedom. Freedom requires that the individual be allowed to pursue *his own* ends: one who is free is in peacetime no longer bound by the common concrete ends of his community. Such freedom of individual decision is made possible by delimiting distinct individual rights (the rights of property, for example) and designating domains within which each can dispose over means known to him for his own ends. That is, a recognisable free sphere is determined for each person. This is all-important. For to have something of one's own, however little, is also the foundation on which a distinctive personality can be formed and a distinctive environment created within which particular individual aims can be pursued.

But confusion has been created by the common supposition that it is possible to have this kind of freedom without restraints. This supposition appears in the *aperçu* ascribed to Voltaire that 'quand je peux faire ce que je veux, voilà la liberté', in Bentham's declaration that 'every law is an evil, for every law is an infraction of liberty' (1789/1887:48), in Bertrand Russell's definition of liberty as the 'absence of obstacles to the realisation of our desires' (1940:251), and in countless other sources. General freedom in this sense is nevertheless impossible, for the freedom of each would founder on the unlimited freedom, i.e., the lack of restraint, of all others.

The question then is how to secure the greatest possible freedom for all. This can be secured by uniformly restricting the freedom of all by abstract rules that preclude arbitrary or discriminatory coercion by or of other people, that prevent any from invading the free sphere of any other (see Hayek 1960 and 1973, and chapter two above). In short, common concrete ends are replaced by common abstract rules. Government is needed only to enforce these abstract rules, and thereby to protect the individual against coercion, or invasion of his free sphere, by others. Whereas enforced obedience to common concrete ends is tantamount to slavery, obedience to common abstract rules (however burdensome they may still feel) provides scope for the most extraordinary freedom and diversity. Although it is sometimes supposed that such diversity brings chaos threatening the relative order that we also associate with civilisation, it turns out that greater diversity brings greater order. Hence the type of liberty made possible by adhering to abstract rules, in contrast to freedom from restraint, is, as Proudhon once put it, 'the mother, not the daughter, of order'.

There is in fact no reason to expect that the selection by evolution of habitual practices should produce happiness. The focus on happiness was introduced by rationalist philosophers who supposed that a conscious reason had to be discovered for the choice of men's morals, and that that reason might prove to be the deliberate pursuit of happiness. But to ask for the conscious reason why man adopted his morals is as mistaken as to ask for what conscious reason man adopted his reason.

Nevertheless, the possibility that the evolved order in which we live provides us with opportunities for happiness that equal or exceed those provided by primitive orders to far fewer people should not be dismissed (which is not to say that such matters can be calculated). Much of the 'alienation' or unhappiness of modern life stems from two sources, one of which affects primarily intellectuals, the other, all beneficiaries of material abundance. The first is a self-fulfilling prophecy of unhappiness for those within any 'system' that does not satisfy rationalistic criteria of conscious control. Thus intellectuals from Rousseau to such recent figures in French and German thought as Foucault and Habermas regard alienation as rampant in any system in which an order is 'imposed' on individuals without their conscious consent; consequently, their followers tend to find civilisation unbearable – by definition, as it were. Secondly, the persistence of instinctual feelings of altruism and solidarity subject those who follow the impersonal rules of the extended order to what is now fashionably called 'bad conscience'; similarly, the acquisition of material success is supposed to be attended with feelings of guilt (or 'social conscience'). In the midst of plenty, then, there is unhappiness not only born of peripheral poverty, but also of the incompatibility, on the part of instinct and of a hubristic reason, with an order that is of a decidedly non-instinctive and extra-rational character.

'Liberation' and Order

On a less sophisticated level than the argument against 'alienation' are the demands for 'liberation' from the burdens of civilisation – including the burdens of disciplined work, responsibility, risk-taking, saving, honesty, the honouring of promises, as well as the difficulties of curbing by general rules one's natural reactions of hostility to strangers and solidarity with those who are like oneself – an ever more severe threat to political liberty. Thus the notion of 'liberation', although allegedly new, is actually archaic in its demand for release from traditional morals. Those who champion such liberation would destroy the basis of freedom, and permit men to do what would irreparably break down those conditions that make civilisation possible. One example appears in so-called 'liberation theology', especially within the Roman Catholic church in South America. But this movement is not confined to South America. Everywhere, in the name of liberation, people disavow practices that enabled mankind to reach its present size and degree of cooperation because they do not *rationally* see, according to their lights, how certain limitations on individual freedom through legal and moral rules make possible a greater – and freer! – order than can be attained through centralised control.

Such demands stem chiefly from the tradition of rationalistic liberalism that we have already discussed (so different from the political liberalism deriving from the English Old Whigs), which implies that freedom is incompatible with any general restriction on individual action. This tradition voices itself in the passages cited earlier from Voltaire, Bentham, and Russell. Unfortunately it also pervades even the work of the English 'saint of rationalism', John Stuart Mill.

Under the influence of these writers, and perhaps especially Mill, the fact that we must purchase the freedom enabling us to form an extended order at the cost of submitting to certain rules of conduct has been used as a justification for the demand to return to the state of 'liberty' enjoyed by the savage who – as eighteenth-century thinkers defined him – 'did not yet know property'. Yet the savage state – which includes the obligation or duty to share in pursuit of the concrete goals of one's fellows, and to obey the commands of a headman – can hardly be described as one of freedom (although it might involve liberation from some particular burdens) or even as one of morals. Only those general and abstract rules that one must take into account in individual decisions in accordance with individual aims deserve the name of morals.

FIVE

THE FATAL CONCEIT

Traditional Morals Fail to Meet Rational Requirements

The four requirements just listed – that whatever is not scientifically proven, or is not fully understood, or lacks a fully specified purpose, or has some unknown effects, is unreasonable – are particularly well suited to constructivist rationalism and to socialist thought. These two approaches themselves flow from a mechanistic or physicalist interpretation of the extended order of human cooperation, that is, from conceiving ordering as the sort of arranging and controlling one could do with a group if one had access to all the facts known to its members. But the extended order is not, and could not be, such an order.

Hence I wish to concede forthwith that most tenets, institutions, and practices of traditional morality and of capitalism do *not* meet the requirements or criteria stated and are – *from the perspective of this theory of reason and science* – 'unreasonable' and 'unscientific'. Moreover, since, as we have also admitted, those who continue to follow traditional practices do not themselves usually understand how these practices were formed or how they endure, it is hardly surprising that alternative 'justifications', so-called, that traditionalists sometimes offer for their practices are often rather naive (and hence have provided fair game for our intellectuals), and have no connection with the real reasons for their success. Many traditionalists do not even bother with justifications that could not be provided anyway (thus allowing intellectuals to denounce them as anti-intellectual or dogmatic), but go on following their practices out of habit or religious faith. Nor is this in any way 'news'. After all, it was over 250 years ago that Hume observed that 'the rules of morality are not the conclusions of our reason'. Yet Hume's claim has not sufficed to deter most modern rationalists from continuing to believe – curiously enough often quoting Hume in their support – that something not derived from reason must be either nonsense or a matter for arbitrary preference, and, accordingly, to continue to demand rational justifications.

Not only the traditional tenets of religion, such as the belief in God, and much traditional morality concerning sex and the family (matters with which I am not concerned in this book), fail to meet these requirements, but also the specific moral traditions that do concern me here, such as private property, saving, exchange, honesty, truthfulness, contract.

The situation may look even worse if one considers that the traditions, institutions and beliefs mentioned not only fail to meet the logical, methodological, and epistemological requirements stated, but that they are also often rejected by socialists on other grounds too. For example, they are seen, as by Chisholm and Keynes, as a 'crippling burden', and also, as by Wells and Forster, as closely associated with despicable trade and commerce (see chapter six). And they also may be seen, as is especially fashionable today, as sources of alienation and oppression, and of 'social injustice'.

After such objections, the conclusion is reached that there is an urgent need to construct a new, rationally revised and justified morality which does meet these requirements, and which is, for that matter, one which will *not* be a crippling burden, be alienating, oppressive, or 'unjust', or be associated with trade. Moreover, this is only part of the great task that these new lawgivers – socialists such as Einstein, Monod and Russell, and self-proclaimed 'immoralists' such as Keynes – set for themselves. A new rational language and law must be constructed too, for existing language and law also fail to meet these requirements, and for what turn out to be the same reasons. (For that matter, even the laws of *science* do not meet these requirements (Hume, 1739/1951; and see Popper, 1934/59).) This awesome task may seem the more urgent to them in that they themselves no longer believe in any supernatural sanction for morality (let alone for language, law, and science) and yet remain convinced that *some* justification is necessary.

So, priding itself on having built its world as if it had designed it, and blaming itself for not having designed it better, humankind is now to set out to do just that. The aim of socialism is no less than to effect a complete redesigning of our traditional morals, law, and language, and on this basis to stamp out the old order and the supposedly inexorable, unjustifiable conditions that prevent the institution of reason, fulfilment, true freedom, and justice.

Justification and Revision of Traditional Morals

The rationalist standards on which this whole argument, indeed this whole programme, rest, are however at best counsels of perfection and at worst the discredited rules of an ancient methodology which may have been incorporated into some of what is thought of as science, but which has nothing to do with real investigation. A highly evolved, rather sophisticated moral system exists side by side, in our extended order, with the primitive theory of rationality and of science sponsored by constructivism, scientism, positivism, hedonism, and socialism. This does not speak against reason and science but against these theories of rationality and science, and some of the practice thereof. All this begins to become evident when it is realised that *nothing* is justifiable in the way demanded. Not only is this so of morals, but also of language and law and even science itself.

> That what I have just written applies to science too may be unfamiliar to some who are not informed of current advances and controversies within the philosophy of science. But it is indeed true not only that our current scientific laws are not justified or justifiable in the way that constructivist methodologists demand, but that we have reason to suppose that we shall eventually learn that many of our present scientific conjectures are untrue. Any conception that guides us more successfully than what we hitherto believed may, moreover, although a great advance, be in substance as mistaken as its predecessor. As we have learnt from Karl Popper (1934/1959), our aim must be to make our successive mistakes as quickly as possible. If we were meanwhile to abandon all present conjectures that we cannot prove to be true, we would soon be back at the level of the savage who trusts only his instincts. Yet this is what all versions of scientism have advised – from Cartesian rationalism to modern positivism.

Moreover, while it is true that *traditional* morals, etc., are not rationally justifiable, this is also true of *any possible moral code, including any that socialists might ever be able to come up with*. Hence no matter what rules we follow, we will not be able to justify them as demanded; so no argument about morals – or science, or law, or language – can legitimately turn on the issue of justification (see Bartley, 1962/1984; 1964, 1982). If we stopped doing everything for which we do not know the reason, or for which we cannot provide a justification in the sense demanded, we would probably very soon be dead.

The issue of justification is indeed a red herring, owing in part to mistaken, and inconsistent, assumptions arising within our main epistemological and methodological tradition which in some cases go back to antiquity. Confusion about justification also stems, particularly so far as the issues that mainly occupy us are concerned, from Auguste Comte, who supposed that we were capable of remaking our moral system as a whole, and replacing it by a completely constructed and justified (or as Comte himself said, 'demonstrated') body of rules.

I shall not state here all the reasons for the irrelevance of traditional demands for justification. But just to take as an example (one appropriate also to the argument of the following section) one popular way of attempting to justify morality, it should be noticed that there is no point to assuming, as rationalist and hedonistic theories of ethics do, that our morality is justified just to the extent, say, that it is directed towards the production of, or striving after, some specific goal such as happiness. There is no reason to suppose that the selection by evolution of such habitual practices as enabled men to nourish larger numbers had much if anything to do with the production of happiness, let alone that it was guided by the striving after it. On the contrary, there is much to indicate that those who aimed simply at happiness would have been overwhelmed by those who just wanted to preserve their lives.

While our moral traditions cannot be constructed, justified or demonstrated in the way demanded, their processes of formation can be partially *re*constructed, and in doing so we can to some degree understand the needs that they serve. To the extent we succeed in this, we are indeed called upon to improve and revise our moral traditions by remedying recognisable defects by piecemeal improvement based on immanent criticism (see Popper, 1945/66, and 1983:29–30), that is, by analysing the compatibility and consistency of their parts, and tinkering with the system accordingly.

As examples of such piecemeal improvement, we have mentioned new contemporary studies of copyright and patents. To take another example, much as we owe to the classical (Roman law) concept of several property as the exclusive right to use or abuse a physical object in any manner we like, it oversimplifies the rules required to maintain an efficient market economy, and a whole new sub-discipline of economics is growing up, devoted to ascertaining how the traditional institution of property can be improved to make the market function better.

What is needed as a preliminary for such analyses includes what is sometimes called a 'rational reconstruction' (using the word 'construction' in a sense very different from 'constructivism') of how the system might have come into being. This is in effect an historical, even natural-historical, investigation, not an attempt to construct, justify, or demonstrate the system itself. It would resemble what followers of Hume used to call 'conjectural history', which tried to make intelligible why some rules rather than others had prevailed (but never overlooked Hume's basic contention, which cannot often enough be repeated, that 'the rules of morality are not the conclusions of our reason'). This is the path taken not only by the Scottish philosophers but by a long chain of students of cultural evolution, from the classical Roman grammarians and linguists, to Bernard Mandeville, through Herder, Giambattista

Vico (who had the profound insight that *homo non intelligendo fit omnia* ('man became all he is without understanding it' (1854: V,183)), and the German historians of law that we have mentioned, such as von Savigny, and on to Carl Menger. Menger was the only one of these to have come after Darwin, yet all attempted to provide a rational reconstruction, conjectural history, or evolutionary account of the emergence of cultural institutions.

At this point I find myself in the embarrassing position of wanting to claim that it must be the members of my own profession, the economists, specialists who understand the process of formation of extended orders, who are most likely to be able to provide explanations of those moral traditions that made the growth of civilisation possible. Only someone who can account for effects such as those connected with several property can explain why this type of practice enabled those groups following it to outstrip others whose morals were better suited to the achievement of different aims. But my desire to plead for my fellow economists, while partly in order, would perhaps be more appropriate were not so many of them themselves infected with constructivism.

How then do morals arise? What is *our* 'rational reconstruction'? We have already sketched it in the foregoing chapters. Apart from the constructivist contention that an adequate morality can be designed and constructed afresh by reason, there are at least two other possible sources of morality. There is, first, as we saw, the innate morality, so-called, of our instincts (solidarity, altruism, group decision, and such like), the practices flowing from which are not sufficient to sustain our present extended order and its population.

Second, there is the evolved morality (savings, several property, honesty, and so on) that created and sustains the extended order. As we have already seen, this morality stands *between* instinct and reason, a position that has been obscured by the false dichotomy of instinct *versus* reason.

The extended order depends on this morality in the sense that it came into being through the fact that those groups following its underlying rules increased in numbers and in wealth relative to other groups. The paradox of our extended order, and of the market – and a stumbling block for socialists and constructivists – is that, through this process, we are able to sustain more from discoverable resources (and indeed in that very process discover more resources) than would be possible by a personally directed process. And although this morality is not 'justified' by the fact that it enables us to do these things, and thereby to survive, *it does enable us to survive, and there is something perhaps to be said for that.*

70

The Limits of Guidance by Factual Knowledge; The Impossibility of Observing the Effects of Our Morality

False assumptions about the possibility of justification, construction or demonstration are perhaps at the root of scientism. But even if they were to understand this, proponents of scientism would undoubtedly want to fall back on the other requirements of their ancient methodology, which are connected to, but are not strictly dependent on, the demand for justification. For example (to hark back to our list of requirements), it would be objected that one *cannot fully understand* traditional morals and how they work; following them *serves no purpose that one can specify fully* in advance; following them *produces effects that are not immediately observable* and hence *cannot be determined to be beneficial* – and which are in any case *not fully known or foreseen*.

In other words, traditional morals do not conform to the second, third, and fourth requirements. These requirements are, as noted, so closely interrelated that one may, after marking their different emphases, treat them together. Thus, briefly to indicate their interconnections, it would be said that one does not understand what one is doing, or what one's purpose is, unless one knows and can specify fully in advance the observable effects of one's action. Action, it is contended, if it is to be rational, must be deliberate and foresighted.

Unless one were to interpret these requirements in so broad and trivial a manner that they would lose all specific practical meaning – as by saying that the understood purpose of the market order, for example, is to produce the beneficial effect of 'generating wealth' – following traditional practices, such as those that generate the market order, clearly does not meet these requirements. I do not believe that any party to our discussion would wish to consider these requirements in so trivial an interpretation; certainly they are not so intended either by their proponents or their opponents. Consequently we may get a clearer view of the situation in which we actually find ourselves by conceding that, indeed, our traditional institutions are not understood, and do not have their purposes or their effects, beneficial or otherwise, specified in advance. And so much the better for them.

In the marketplace (as in other institutions of our extended order), unintended consequences are paramount: a distribution of resources is effected by an impersonal process in which individuals, acting for their own ends (themselves also often rather vague), literally do not and cannot know what will be the net result of their interactions.

Take the requirements that it is unreasonable to follow or do anything blindly (i.e., without understanding) and that the purposes and *effects* of a proposed action must not only be fully known in advance

71

but also fully observable and maximally beneficial. Now apply these requirements to the notion of an extended order. When we consider this order in the vast evolutionary frame in which it developed, the absurdity of the demands becomes evident. The decisive effects that led to the creation of the order itself, and to certain practices predominating over others, were exceedingly remote results of what earlier individuals had done, results exerting themselves on groups of which earlier individuals could hardly have been aware, and which effects, had earlier individuals been able to know them, may *not* have appeared at all beneficial to them, whatever later individuals may think. As for those later individuals, there is no reason why all (or any) of *them* should be endowed with a full knowledge of history, let alone of evolutionary theory, economics, and everything else they would have to know, so as to perceive why the group whose practices they follow should have flourished more than others – although no doubt some persons are always adept at inventing justifications of current or local practice. Many of the evolved rules which secured greater cooperation and prosperity for the extended order may have differed utterly from anything that could have been anticipated, and might even seem repugnant to someone or other, *earlier or later* in the evolution of that order. In the extended order, the *circumstances* determining what each must do to achieve his own ends include, conspicuously, unknown decisions of many other unknown people about what means to use for *their* own purposes. Hence, at no moment in the process could individuals have designed, according to their purposes, the functions of the rules that gradually did form the order; and only later, and imperfectly and retrospectively, have we been able to begin to explain these formations *in principle* (see Hayek, 1967, essays 1 and 2).

There is no ready English or even German word that precisely characterises an extended order, or how its way of functioning contrasts with the rationalists' requirements. The only appropriate word, 'transcendent', has been so misused that I hesitate to use it. In its literal meaning, however, it does concern that which *far surpasses the reach of our understanding, wishes and purposes, and our sense perceptions*, and that which incorporates and generates knowledge which no individual brain, or any single organisation, could possess or invent. This is conspicuously so in its religious meaning, as we see for example in the Lord's Prayer, where it is asked that '*Thy* will [i.e., not *mine*] be done in earth as it is in heaven'; or in the Gospel, where it is declared: 'Ye have not chosen me but I have chosen you, that ye should go and bring forth fruit, and that your fruit should remain' (St. John, 15:26). But a more purely transcendent ordering, which also happens to be a purely naturalistic ordering (not derived from any supernatural power), as for example in evolution, abandons the animism still present in religion: the idea that a single brain or will (as for example, that of an omniscient God) could control and order.

The rejection of rationalistic requirements on grounds such as these thus also has an important consequence for anthropomorphism and animism of all sorts – and thus for socialism. If market coordination of individual activities, as well as other moral traditions and institutions, results from natural, spontaneous, and self-ordering processes of adaptation to a greater number of particular facts than any one mind can perceive or even conceive, it is evident that demands that these processes be just, or possess other moral attributes (see chapter seven), derive from a naive anthropomorphism. Such demands of course might be appropriately addressed to the directors of a process guided by rational control or to a god attentive to prayers, but are wholly inappropriate to the impersonal self-ordering process actually at work.

In an order so extended as to transcend the comprehension and possible guidance of any single mind, a unified will can indeed hardly determine the welfare of its several members in terms of some particular conception of justice, or according to an agreed scale. Nor is this due merely to the problems of anthropomorphism. It is also because 'welfare . . . has no principle, neither for him who receives it, nor for him who distributes it (one places it here, another there); because it depends on the material content of the will, which is dependent on particular facts and therefore is incapable of a general rule' (Kant, 1798:II, 6, note 2). The insight that general rules must prevail for spontaneity to flourish, as reaped by Hume and Kant, has never been refuted, merely neglected or forgotten.

Although 'welfare has no principle' – and hence cannot generate spontaneous order – resistance to those rules of justice that made the extended order possible, and denunciation of them as anti-moral, stem from the belief that welfare *must* have a principle, and from refusal (and here is where anthropomorphism reenters the picture) to accept that the extended order arises out of a competitive process in which success decides, not approval of a great mind, a committee, or a god, or conformity with some understood principle of individual merit. In this order the advance of some is paid for by the failure of equally sincere and even meritorious endeavours of others. Reward is not for merit (e.g., obedience to moral rules, cf. Hayek 1960:94). For instance, we may fulfil the needs of others, regardless of their merit or the reason for our ability to fulfil them. As Kant saw, no common standard of merit can judge between different opportunities open to different individuals with

73

different information, different abilities, and different desires. This latter situation is indeed the usual one. Discoveries enabling some to prevail are mostly unintended or unforeseen – by those who prevail as well as by those who fail. The value of products resulting from necessary changes of individual activities will rarely seem just since they are made necessary by unforeseen events. Nor can the steps of a process of evolution towards what was previously unknown appear just in the sense of conforming to preconceptions of rightness and wrongness, of 'welfare', or of possibilities open in circumstances *previously* obtaining.

Understandable aversion to such morally blind results, results inseparable from any process of trial-and-error, leads men to want to achieve a contradiction in terms: namely, to wrest control of evolution – i.e., of the procedure of trial and error – and to shape it to their present wishes. But invented moralities resulting from this reaction give rise to irreconcilable claims that no system can satisfy and which thus remain the source of unceasing conflict. The fruitless attempt *to render a situation just* whose outcome, by its nature, cannot be determined by what anyone does or can know, only damages the functioning of the process itself.

Such demands for justice are simply inappropriate to a naturalistic evolutionary process – inappropriate not just to what has happened in the past, but to what is going on at present. For of course this evolutionary process is still at work. Civilisation is not only a product of evolution – it is a process; by establishing a framework of general rules and individual freedom it allows itself to continue to evolve. This evolution cannot be guided by and often will not produce what men demand. Men may find some previously unfulfilled wishes satisfied, but only at the price of disappointing many others. Though by moral conduct an individual may increase his opportunities, the resulting evolution will not gratify all his moral desires. *Evolution cannot be just.*

Indeed, to insist that all future change be just would be to demand that evolution come to a halt. Evolution leads us ahead precisely in bringing about much that we could not intend or foresee, let alone prejudge for its moral properties. One only need ask (particularly in light of the historical account given in chapters two and three) what would have been the effect if, at some earlier date, some magic force had been granted the power to enforce, say, some egalitarian or meritocratic creed. One soon recognises that such an event would have made the evolution of civilisation impossible. A Rawlsian world (Rawls, 1971) could thus never have become civilised: by repressing differentiation due to luck, it would have scotched most discoveries of new possibilities. In such a world we would be deprived of those signals that alone can tell each what, as a result of thousands of changes in the conditions in

74

which we live, we must now do in order to keep the stream of production flowing and, if possible, increasing.

Intellectuals may of course claim to have invented new and better 'social' morals that will accomplish just this, but these 'new' rules represent a recidivism to the morals of the primitive micro-order, and can hardly maintain the life and health of the billions supported by the macro-order.

It is easy to understand anthropomorphism, even though we must reject it for its mistakes. And this brings us back to the positive and sympathetic aspect of the standpoint of the intellectuals whose views we have contested. Man's inventiveness contributed so much to the formation of super-individual structures within which individuals found great opportunities that people came to imagine that they could deliberately design the whole as well as some of its parts, and that the mere existence of such extended structures shows that they can be deliberately designed. Although this is an error, it is a noble one, one that is, in Mises's words, 'grandiose . . . ambitious . . . magnificent . . . daring'.

Unspecified Purposes: In the Extended Order Most Ends of Action Are Not Conscious or Deliberate

There are a number of distinct points and questions, mostly elaborations of what has just been stated, that help make clearer how these matters work together.

First, there is the question of *how our knowledge really does arise*. Most knowledge – and I confess it took me some time to recognise this – is obtained not from immediate experience or observation, but in the continuous process of sifting a learnt tradition, which requires individual recognition and following of moral traditions that are not justifiable in terms of the canons of traditional theories of rationality. The tradition is the product of a process of selection from among irrational, or, rather, 'unjustified' beliefs which, without anyone's knowing or intending it, assisted the proliferation of those who followed them (with no necessary relationship to the reasons – as for example religious reasons – for which they were followed). The process of selection that shaped customs and morality could take account of more factual circumstances than individuals could perceive, and in consequence tradition is in some respects superior to, or 'wiser' than, human reason (see chapter one above). This decisive insight is one that only a *very* critical rationalist could recognise.

75

Second, and closely related to this, there is the question raised earlier of what, in the evolutionary selection of rules of conduct, is really decisive. The immediately perceived effects of actions that humans tend to concentrate on are fairly unimportant to this selection; rather, selection is made according to the consequences of the decisions guided by the rules of conduct in the long run – the same long run sneered at by Keynes (1971, *C.W.*:IV, 65). These consequences depend – as argued above and discussed again below – chiefly on rules of property and contract securing the personal domain of the individual. Hume had already noticed this, writing that these rules 'are not derived from any utility or advantage which either the *particular* person or the public may reap from his enjoyment of any *particular* good' (1739/1886:II, 273). Men did not foresee the benefits of rules before adopting them, though some people gradually have become aware of what they owe to the whole system.

Our earlier claim, that acquired traditions serve as 'adaptations to the unknown', must then be taken literally. Adaptation to the unknown is the key in all evolution, and the totality of events to which the modern market order constantly adapts itself is indeed unknown to anybody. The information that individuals or organisations can use to adapt to the unknown is necessarily partial, and is conveyed by signals (e.g., prices) through long chains of individuals, each person passing on in modified form a combination of streams of abstract market signals. Nonetheless, *the whole structure of activities tends to adapt, through these partial and fragmentary signals, to conditions foreseen by and known to no individual*, even if this adaptation is never perfect. That is why this structure survives, and why those who use it also survive and prosper.

There can be no deliberately planned substitutes for such a self-ordering process of adaptation to the unknown. Neither his reason nor his innate 'natural goodness' leads man this way, only the bitter necessity of submitting to rules he does not like in order to maintain himself against competing groups that had already begun to expand because they stumbled such rules earlier.

If we had deliberately built, or were consciously shaping, the structure of human action, we would merely have to ask individuals why they had interacted with any particular structure. Whereas, in fact, specialised students, even after generations of effort, find it exceedingly difficult to explain such matters, and cannot agree on what are the causes or what will be the effects of particular events. The curious task of economics is to demonstrate to men how little they really know about what they imagine they can design.

To the naive mind that can conceive of order only as the product of deliberate arrangement, it may seem absurd that in complex conditions order, and adaptation to the unknown, can be achieved more effectively by decentralising decisions, and that a division of authority will actually extend the possibility of overall order. Yet that decentralisation actually leads to more information being taken into account. This is the main reason for rejecting the requirements of constructivist rationalism. For the same reason, only the alterable division of the power of disposal over particular resources among many individuals actually able to decide on their use – a division obtained through individual freedom and several property – makes the fullest exploitation of dispersed knowledge possible.

Much of the particular information which any individual possesses can be used only to the extent to which he himself can use it in his own decisions. Nobody can communicate to another all that he knows, because much of the information he can make use of he himself will elicit only in the process of making plans for action. Such information will be evoked as he works upon the particular task he has undertaken in the conditions in which he finds himself, such as the relative scarcity of various materials to which he has access. Only thus can the individual find out what to look for, and what helps him to do this in the market is the responses others make to what they find in their own environments. The overall problem is not merely to make use of given knowledge, but to discover as much information as is worth searching for in prevailing conditions.

It is often objected that the institution of property is selfish in that it benefits only those who own some, and that it was indeed 'invented' by some persons who, having acquired some individual possessions, wished for their exclusive benefit to protect these from others. Such notions, which of course underlie Rousseau's resentment, and his allegation that our 'shackles' have been imposed by selfish and exploitative interests, fail to take into account that the size of our overall product is so large only because we can, through market exchange of severally owned property, use widely dispersed knowledge of particular facts to allocate severally owned resources. The market is the only known method of providing information enabling individuals to judge comparative advantages of different uses of resources of which they have immediate knowledge and through whose use, whether they so intend or not, they serve the needs of distant unknown individuals. This dispersed knowledge is *essentially* dispersed, and cannot possibly be gathered together and conveyed to an authority charged with the task of deliberately creating order.

Thus the institution of several property is not selfish, nor was it, nor could it have been, 'invented' to impose the will of property-owners upon the rest. Rather, it is generally beneficial in that it transfers the

77

guidance of production from the hands of a few individuals who, whatever they may pretend, have limited knowledge, to a process, the extended order, that makes maximum use of the knowledge of all, thereby benefiting those who do not own property nearly as much as those who do.

Nor does freedom of all under the law require that *all* be able to own individual property but that *many* people do so. I myself should certainly prefer to be without property in a land in which many others own something, than to have to live where all property is 'collectively owned' and assigned by authority to particular uses.

But this argument too is challenged, even ridiculed, as the selfish excuse of privileged classes. Intellectuals, thinking in terms of limited causal processes they had learnt to interpret in areas such as physics, found it easy to persuade manual workers that selfish decisions of individual owners of capital – rather than the market process itself – made use of widely dispersed opportunities and constantly changing relevant facts. The whole process of calculating in terms of market prices was, indeed, sometimes even represented as part of a devious manoeuvre on the part of owners of capital to conceal how they exploited workers. But such retorts quite fail to address the arguments and facts already rehearsed: *some hypothetical body of objective facts is no more available to capitalists for manipulating the whole than it is to the managers that the socialists would like to replace them.* Such objective facts simply do not exist and are unavailable to anyone.

Third, there is a *difference between following rules of conduct, on the one hand, and knowledge about something, on the other* (a difference pointed to by various persons in various ways, for instance by Gilbert Ryle in his distinction between 'knowing how' and 'knowing that' (1945–46:1–16; 1949)). The habit of following rules of conduct is an ability utterly different from the knowledge that one's actions will have certain kinds of effects. This conduct ought to be seen for what it is, the skill to fit oneself into, or align oneself with, a pattern of whose very existence one may barely be aware and of whose ramifications one has scarcely any knowledge. Most people can, after all, recognise and adapt themselves to several different patterns of conduct without being able to explain or describe them. How one responds to perceived events would thus by no means necessarily be determined by knowledge of the effects of one's own actions, for we often do not and cannot have such knowledge. If we cannot have it, there is hardly anything rational about the demand that we *ought* to have it; and indeed we should be the poorer if what we did were guided solely by the limited knowledge that we do have of such effects.

A pre-formation of an order or pattern in a brain or mind is not only *not* a superior but an inferior method of securing an order. For it must always be a small part of the overall system in which some features of that larger system can reflect themselves. As little as it is possible for the human brain ever fully to explain itself (Hayek, 1952:8.66–8.86) is it possible for that brain to account for, or predict, the result of the interaction of a large number of human brains.

Fourth, there is the important point that *an order arising from the separate decisions of many individuals on the basis of different information cannot be determined by a common scale of the relative importance of different ends.* This brings us close to the issue of marginal utility, an important matter that we shall postpone discussing until chapter six. Here, however, it is appropriate to discuss in a general way the advantages of the differentiation that an extended order makes possible. Freedom involves freedom to be different – to have one's own ends in one's own domain; yet order everywhere, and not only in human affairs, also presupposes differentiation of its elements. Such differentiation might be confined merely to the local or temporal position of its elements, but an order would hardly be of any interest unless the differences were greater than this. Order is desirable not for keeping everything in place but for generating new powers that would otherwise not exist. The degree of orderliness – the new powers that order creates and confers – depends more on the variety of the elements than on their temporal or local position.

Illustrations are everywhere. Consider how genetic evolution favoured the unique extension of the infancy and childhood of humankind because that made possible extremely great diversity, and thereby a great acceleration of cultural evolution and a quickening of the increase of the species *homo*. Though biologically determined differences among individual men are probably smaller than those of some domesticated animals (especially dogs), this long learning period after birth allows individuals more time to adapt themselves to particular environments and to absorb the different streams of tradition into which they are born. The varieties of skills that make division of labour possible, and with it the extended order, are largely due to these different streams of tradition, encouraged by underlying dissimilarities in natural gifts and preferences. The whole of tradition is, moreover, so incomparably more complex than what any individual mind can command that it can be transmitted at all only if there are many different individuals to absorb different portions of it. The advantage of individual differentiation is all the greater in that it makes large groups more efficient.

Thus, differences among individuals increase the power of the collaborating group beyond the sum of individual efforts. Synergetic collaboration brings into play distinctive talents that would have been left unused had their possessors been forced to strive alone for sustenance. Specialisation releases and encourages the development of a few individuals whose distinctive contributions may suffice to provide them a living or even to exceed the contributions others make to the total. Civilisation is, in the famous phrase of Wilhelm von Humboldt which Stuart Mill placed on the title page of his essay *On Liberty*, based on 'human development in its richest diversity'.

The knowledge that plays probably the chief role in this differentiation – far from being the knowledge of any one human being, let alone that of a directing superbrain – arises in a process of experimental interaction of widely dispersed, different and even conflicting beliefs of millions of communicating individuals. The increasing intelligence shown by man is, accordingly, due not so much to increases in the several knowledge of individuals but to procedures for combining different and scattered information which, in turn, generate order and enhance productivity.

Thus the development of variety is an important part of cultural evolution, and a great part of an individual's value to others is due to his differences from them. The importance and value of order will grow with the variety of the elements, while greater order in turn enhances the value of variety, and thus the order of human cooperation becomes indefinitely extensible. If things were otherwise, if for example all men were alike and could not make themselves different from one another, there would be little point in division of labour (except perhaps among people in different localities), little advantage from coordinating efforts, and little prospect of creating order of any power or magnitude.

Thus individuals had to become different before they could be free to combine into complex structures of cooperation. Moreover, they had to combine into entities of a distinct character: not merely a sum but a structure in some manner analogous to, and in some important respects differing from, an organism.

Fifth, there is the question *whence then, in the presence of all these difficulties and objections, the demand to restrict one's action to the deliberate pursuit of known and observable beneficial ends arises.* It is in part a remnant of the instinctual, and cautious, micro-ethic of the small band, wherein jointly perceived purposes were directed to the visible needs of personally known comrades (i.e., solidarity and altruism). Earlier I claimed that, within an extended order, solidarity and altruism are possible only in a limited way within some sub-groups, and that to restrict the behaviour of the group at large to such action would work against coordinating the efforts of its members. Once most of the productive activities of members of a cooperating group transcend the range of the individual's perception, the old impulse to follow inborn altruistic instincts actually hinders the formation of more extensive orders.

In the sense of inculcating conduct that benefits others, all systems of morality of course commend altruistic action; but the question is how to accomplish this. Good intentions will not suffice – we all know what road they pave. Guidance strictly by perceivable favourable effects on particular other persons is insufficient for, and even irreconcilable with, the extended order. The morals of the market do lead us to benefit others, not by our intending to do so, but by making us act in a manner which, nonetheless, will have just that effect. The extended order *circumvents* individual ignorance (and thus also adapts us to the unknown, as discussed above) in a way that good intentions alone cannot do – and thereby does make our efforts altruistic in their effects.

In an order taking advantage of the higher productivity of extensive division of labour, the individual can no longer know whose needs his efforts do or ought to serve, or what will be the effects of his actions on those unknown persons who do consume his products or products to which he has contributed. Directing his productive efforts altruistically thus becomes literally impossible for him. In so far as we can still call his motives altruistic in that they eventually redound to the benefit of others, they will do this not because he aims at or intends to serve the concrete needs of others, but because he observes abstract rules. Our 'altruism', in this new sense, is very different from instinctual altruism. No longer the end pursued but the rules observed make the action good or bad. Observing these rules, while bending most of our efforts towards earning a living, enables us to confer benefits beyond the range of our concrete knowledge (yet at the same time hardly prevents us from using whatever extra we earn also to gratify our instinctive longing to do visible good). All this is obscured by the systematic abuse of the term 'altruistic' by sociobiologists.

Another explanation for the demand that one's actions be restricted to the deliberate pursuit of known beneficial ends may also be mentioned. The demand arises not only from archaic and uninstructed instinct but also from a characteristic peculiar to those intellectuals who champion it – an entirely understandable characteristic which nonetheless remains self-defeating. Intellectuals are especially anxious to know for what ultimate purpose what they themselves call their 'brain children' will be used, and thus passionately concern themselves with the fate of their ideas, and hesitate much more to release thoughts from their control than do manual workers their material products. This reaction often makes such highly educated people reluctant to integrate

81

themselves into the exchange processes, processes that involve working for unperceivable ends in a situation where the only *identifiable* result of their efforts, if any, may indeed be someone else's profit. The manual worker readily assumes that it is indeed his employer's job to know, if anyone does, what needs the work of his hands will ultimately satisfy. But the place of individual intellectual work in the *product* of many intellectuals interacting in a chain of services or ideas will be less identifiable. That better educated people should be more reluctant to submit to some unintelligible direction – such as the market (despite their talk of the 'marketplace of ideas') – thus has the result (also unintended) that they tend to resist just what (without their understanding it) would increase their usefulness to their fellows.

This reluctance helps further to explain the hostility intellectuals bear towards the market order, and something of their susceptibility to socialism. Perhaps this hostility and susceptibility would diminish if such persons understood better the role that abstract and spontaneous ordering patterns play in all of life, as they no doubt would do if better informed of evolution, biology, and economics. But when confronted by information in these fields, they often are reluctant to listen, or even to consider conceding the existence of complex entities of whose working our minds can have only abstract knowledge. For mere abstract knowledge of the general structure of such entities is insufficient to enable us literally to 'build' them (that is, to put them together from known pieces), or to predict the particular form they will assume. At best, it can indicate under what general conditions many such orders or systems will form themselves, conditions that we may sometimes be able to create. This sort of problem is familiar to the chemist concerned with similarly complex phenomena but usually unfamiliar to the kind of scientist accustomed to explaining everything in terms of simple connections between a few observable events. The result is that such persons are tempted to interpret more complex structures animistically as the result of design, and to suspect some secret and dishonest manipulation – some conspiracy, as of a dominant 'class' – behind 'designs' whose designers are nowhere to be found. This in turn helps to reinforce their initial reluctance to relinquish control of their own products in a market order. For intellectuals generally, the feeling of being mere tools of concealed, even if impersonal, market forces appears almost as a personal humiliation.

It evidently has not occurred to them that the capitalists who are suspected of directing it all are actually also tools of an impersonal process, just as unaware of the ultimate effects and purpose of their actions, but merely concerned with a higher level, and therefore a wider range, of events in the whole structure. Moreover, the idea that the question whether their own ends are satisfied should depend on the activities of *such* men – men concerned solely with means – is itself an abomination to them.

The Ordering of the Unknown

The English language unfortunately lacks a popular word available in German: namely, *Machbarkeit*. I sometimes wonder whether a good cause might not be served by coining an equivalent English term 'makeability' – 'manufacturability' does not quite do (and my own 'constructivism' could hardly be rendered by 'constructible') – to describe the view that we have confronted, examined and contested throughout this chapter and the last: namely, that anything produced by evolution could have been done better by the use of human ingenuity.

This view is untenable. For in fact we are able to bring about an ordering of the unknown *only by causing it to order itself*. In dealing with our physical surroundings we sometimes can indeed achieve our ends by relying on the self-ordering forces of nature, but not by deliberately trying to arrange elements in the order that we wish them to assume. This is for example what we do when we initiate processes that produce crystals or new chemical substances (see previous section and also Appendix C). In chemistry, and even more in biology, we must use self-ordering processes in an increasing measure; we can create the conditions under which they will operate, but we cannot determine what will happen to any particular element. Most synthetic chemical compounds are not 'constructible' in the sense that we can create them by placing the individual elements composing them in the appropriate places. All we can do is to induce their formation.

A similar procedure must be followed to initiate processes that will coordinate individual actions transcending our observation. In order to induce the self-formation of certain abstract structures of inter-personal relations, we need to secure the assistance of some very general conditions, and then allow each individual element to find its own place within the larger order. The most we can do to assist the process is to admit only such elements as obey the required rules. This limitation of our powers necessarily grows with the complexity of the structure that we wish to bring into being.

An individual who finds himself at some point in an extended order where only his immediate environment is known to him can apply this advice to his own situation. He may need to start by trying continuously to probe beyond the limits of what he can see, in order to establish and maintain the communication that creates and sustains the overall order.

Indeed, maintaining communication within the order requires that dispersed information be utilised by many different individuals, unknown to one another, in a way that allows the different knowledge of millions to form an exosomatic or material pattern. Every individual becomes a link in many chains of transmission through which he receives signals enabling him to adapt his plans to circumstances he does not know. The overall order thus becomes infinitely expansible, spontaneously supplying information about an increasing range of means without exclusively serving particular ends.

Earlier, we considered some important aspects of such processes of communication, including the market with its necessary and continual variation of prices. Here it need only be added and stressed that, beyond regulating current production of commodities and supplies of services, the same traditions and practices also provide for the future; their effects will manifest themselves not only as an interlocal order, but also as an intertemporal one. Actions will be adapted not only to others distant in space but also to events beyond the life expectancies of acting individuals. Only a confessed immoralist could indeed defend measures of policy on the grounds that 'in the long run we are all dead'. For the only groups to have spread and developed are those among whom it became customary to try to provide for children and later descendants whom one might never see.

Some persons are so troubled by some effects of the market order that they overlook how unlikely and even wonderful it is to find such an order prevailing in the greater part of the modern world, a world in which we find thousands of millions of people working in a constantly changing environment, providing means of subsistence for others who are mostly unknown to them, and at the same time finding satisfied their own expectations that they themselves will receive goods and services produced by equally unknown people. Even in the worst of times something like nine out of ten of them will find these expectations confirmed.

Such an order, although far from perfect and often inefficient, can extend farther than any order men could create by deliberately putting countless elements into selected 'appropriate' places. Most defects and inefficiencies of such spontaneous orders result from attempting to interfere with or to prevent their mechanisms from operating, or to improve the details of their results. Such attempts to intervene in spontaneous order rarely result in anything closely corresponding to men's wishes, since these orders are determined by more particular facts than any such intervening agency can know. Yet, while deliberate intervention to, say, flatten out inequalities in the interest of a random member of the order risks damaging the working of the whole, the self-ordering process will secure for any random member of such a group a better chance over a wider range of opportunities available to all than any rival system could offer.

How What Cannot Be Known Cannot Be Planned

Where has the discussion of our last two chapters brought us? The doubts Rousseau cast on the institution of several property became the foundation of socialism and have continued to influence some of the greatest thinkers of our century. Even as great a figure as Bertrand Russell defined liberty as the 'absence of obstacles to the realisation of our desires' (1940:251). At least before the obvious economic failure of Eastern European socialism, it was widely thought by such rationalists that a centrally planned economy would deliver not only 'social justice' (see chapter seven below), but also a more efficient use of economic resources. This notion appears eminently sensible at first glance. But it proves to overlook the facts just reviewed: that the totality of resources that one could employ in such a plan *is simply not knowable to anybody*, and therefore can hardly be centrally controlled.

Nonetheless, socialists continue to fail to face the obstacles in the way of fitting separate individual decisions into a common pattern conceived as a 'plan'. The conflict between our instincts, which, since Rousseau, have become identified with 'morality', and the moral traditions that have survived cultural evolution and serve to restrain these instincts, is embodied in the separation now often drawn between certain sorts of ethical and political philosophy on the one hand and economics on the other. The point is not that whatever economists determine to be efficient is therefore 'right', but that economic analysis can elucidate the usefulness of practices heretofore thought to be right – usefulness from the perspective of any philosophy that looks unfavourably on the human suffering and death that would follow the collapse of our civilisation. It is a betrayal of concern for others, then, to theorise about the 'just society' without carefully considering the economic consequences of implementing such views. Yet, after seventy years of experience with socialism, it is safe to say that most intellectuals outside the areas – Eastern Europe and the Third World – where socialism has been tried remain content to brush aside what lessons might lie in economics, unwilling to wonder whether there might not be a *reason* why socialism, as often as it is attempted, never seems to work out as its intellectual leaders *intended*. The intellectuals' vain search for a truly socialist community, which results in the idealisation of, and then disillusion-

85

ment with, a seemingly endless string of 'utopias' – the Soviet Union, then Cuba, China, Yugoslavia, Vietnam, Tanzania, Nicaragua – should suggest that there might be something about socialism that does not conform to certain facts. But such facts, first explained by economists more than a century ago, remain unexamined by those who pride themselves on their rationalistic rejection of the notion that there could be any facts that transcend historical context or present an insurmountable barrier to human desires.

Meanwhile, among those who, in the tradition of Mandeville, Hume, and Smith, did study economics, there gradually emerged not only an understanding of market processes, but a powerful critique of the possibility of substituting socialism for them. The advantages of these market procedures were so contrary to expectation that they could be explained only retrospectively, through analysing this spontaneous formation itself. When this was done, it was found that decentralised control over resources, control through several property, leads to the generation and use of more information than is possible under central direction. Order and control extending beyond the immediate purview of any central authority could be attained by central direction only if, contrary to fact, those local managers who could gauge visible and potential resources were *also* currently informed of the constantly changing relative importance of such resources, and could then communicate full and accurate details about this to some central planning authority in time for it to tell them what to do in the light of all the other, different, concrete information it had received from other regional or local managers – who of course, in turn, found themselves in similar difficulties in obtaining and delivering any such information.

Once we realise what the task of such a central planning authority would be, it becomes clear that the commands it would have to issue could not be derived from the information the local managers had recognised as important, but could only be determined through direct dealings among individuals or groups controlling clearly delimited aggregates of means. The hypothetical assumption, customarily employed in theoretical descriptions of the market process (descriptions made by people who usually have no intention of supporting socialism), to the effect that all such facts (or 'parameters') can be assumed to be known to the explaining theorist, obscures all this, and consequently produces the curious deceptions that help to sustain various forms of socialist thinking.

The order of the extended economy is, and can be, formed only by a wholly different process – from an evolved method of communication that makes it possible to transmit, not an infinite multiplicity of reports about particular facts, but merely certain abstract properties of several particular conditions, such as competitive prices, which must be brought into mutual correspondence to achieve overall order. These communicate the different rates of substitution or equivalence that the several parties involved find prevailing between the various goods and services whose use they command. Certain quantities of any such objects may prove to be equivalents or possible substitutes for one another, either for satisfying particular human needs or for producing, directly or indirectly, means to satisfy them. Surprising as it may be that such a process exists at all, let alone that it came into being through evolutionary selection without being deliberately designed, I know of no efforts to refute this contention or discredit the process itself – unless one so regards simple declarations that all such facts can, somehow, be known to some central planning authority. (See also, in this connection, the discussion of economic calculation, in Babbage (1832), Gossen (1854/1889/1927), Pierson (1902/1912), Mises (1922/81), Hayek (1935), Rutland (1985), Roberts (1971).)

Indeed the whole idea of 'central control' is confused. There is not, and never could be, a single directing mind at work; there will always be some council or committee charged with designing a plan of action for some enterprise. Though individual members may occasionally, to convince the others, quote particular pieces of information that have influenced their views, the conclusions of the body will generally not be based on common knowledge but on agreement among several views based on different information. Each bit of knowledge contributed by one person will tend to lead some other to recall yet other facts of whose relevance he has become aware only by his being told of yet other circumstances of which he did not know. Such a process thus remains one of making use of dispersed knowledge (and thus simulates trading, although in a highly inefficient way – a way usually lacking competition and diminished in accountability), rather than unifying the knowledge of a number of persons. The members of the group will be able to communicate to one another few of their distinct reasons; they will communicate chiefly conclusions drawn from their respective individual knowledge of the problem in hand. Moreover, only rarely will circumstances really be the same for different persons contemplating the same situation – at least in so far as this concerns some sector of the extended order and not merely a more or less self-contained group.

Perhaps the best illustration of the impossibility of deliberate 'rational' allocation of resources in an extended economic order without the guidance by prices formed in competitive markets is the problem of allocating the current supply of liquid capital among all the different uses whereby it could increase the final product. The problem is essentially how much of the currently accruing productive resources can be spared to provide for the more distant future as against present needs. Adam Smith was aware of the representative character of this

87

issue when, referring to the problem faced by an individual owner of such capital, he wrote: 'What is the species of domestick industry which his capital can employ, and of which the produce is likely to be of the greatest value, every individual, it is evident, can, in his local situation, judge much better than any statesman or lawgiver can do for him' (1776/1976).

> If we consider the problem of the use of all means available for investment in an extended economic system under a single directing authority, the first difficulty is that no such determinate aggregate quantity of capital available for current use can be known to anyone, although of course this quantity is limited in the sense that the effect of investing either more or less than it must lead to discrepancies between the demand for various kinds of goods and services. Such discrepancies will not be self-correcting but will manifest themselves through some of the instructions given by the directing authority proving to be impossible of execution, either because some of the goods required will not be there or because some materials or instruments provided cannot be used due to the lack of required complementary means (tools, materials, or labour). None of the magnitudes that would have to be taken into account could be ascertained by inspecting or measuring any 'given' objects, but all will depend on possibilities among which other persons will have to choose in the light of knowledge that they possess at the time. An approximate solution of this task will become possible only by the interplay of those who can ascertain particular circumstances which the conditions of the moment show, through their effects on market prices, to be relevant. The 'quantity of capital' available then proves, for example, what happens when the share of current resources used to provide for needs in the more distant future is greater than what people are prepared to spare from current consumption in order to increase provision for that future, i.e., their willingness to save.

Comprehending the role played by the transmission of information (or of factual knowledge) opens the door to understanding the extended order. Yet these issues are highly abstract, and are particularly hard to grasp for those schooled in the mechanistic, scientistic, constructivist canons of rationality that dominate our educational systems – and who consequently tend to be ignorant of biology, economics, and evolution. I confess that it took me too a long time from my first breakthrough, in my essay on 'Economics and Knowledge' (1936/48), through the recognition of 'Competition as a Discovery Procedure' (1978:179–190), and my essay on 'The Pretence of Knowledge' (1978:23–34), to state my theory of the dispersal of information, from which follows my conclusions about the superiority of spontaneous formations to central direction.

SIX

THE MYSTERIOUS WORLD OF TRADE
AND MONEY

Disdain for the Commercial

Not all antipathy to the market order arises from questions of epistemology, methodology, rationality and science. There is a further, darker, dislike. To understand it, we must step behind these relatively rational areas to something more archaic and even arcane: to attitudes and emotions that arise especially powerfully when commercial activity, trade and financial institutions are discussed by socialists – or encountered by primitives.

As we have seen, trade and commerce often depend importantly on confidentiality, as well as on specialised or individual knowledge; and this is even more so of financial institutions. In commercial activities, for example, more is at risk than one's own time and effort, and special information enables individuals to judge their chances, their competitive edge, in particular ventures. Knowledge of special circumstances is only worth striving for if its possession confers some advantage compensating for the cost of acquiring it. If every trader had to make public how and where to obtain better or cheaper wares, so that all his competitors could at once imitate him, it would hardly be worth his while to engage in the process at all – and the benefits accruing from trade would never arise. Moreover, so much knowledge of particular circumstances is unarticulated, and hardly even articulable (for example, an entrepreneur's hunch that a new product might be successful) that it would prove impossible to make it 'public' quite apart from considerations of motivation.

Of course action in accordance with what is not perceived by all and fully specified in advance – what Ernst Mach called the 'observable and tangible' – violates the rationalist requirements discussed earlier. Moreover, what is intangible is also often an object of distrust and even fear. (It may be mentioned in passing that not only socialists fear (if for somewhat different reasons) the circumstances and conditions of trade. Bernard Mandeville 'shuddered' when confronted by 'the most frightful prospect [which] is left behind when we reflect on the toil and hazard that are undergone abroad, the vast seas we are to go over, the different

89

climates we are to endure, and the several nations we must be obliged to for their assistance' (1715/1924:I, 356). To become aware that we depend heavily on human efforts that we cannot know about or control is indeed unnerving – to those who engage in them as well as those who would refrain.)

Such distrust and fear have, since antiquity and in many parts of the world, led ordinary people as well as socialist thinkers to regard trade not only as distinct from material production, not only as chaotic and superfluous in itself, not only as a methodological mistake, as it were, but also as suspicious, inferior, dishonest, and contemptible. Throughout history 'merchants were objects of very general disdain and moral opprobrium . . . a man who bought cheap and sold dear was fundamentally dishonest. . . . Merchant behaviour violated patterns of mutuality that prevailed within primary groupings' (McNeill, 1981:35). As I recall Eric Hoffer once remarking: 'The hostility, in particular of the scribe, towards the merchant is as old as recorded history'.

There are many reasons for such attitudes, and many forms in which they express themselves. Often, in early days, traders were set apart from the rest of the community. Nor was this so only of them. Even some handiworkers, especially blacksmiths, suspected of sorcery by tillers of the soil and herdsmen, were often kept outside the village. After all, did not the smiths, with their 'mysteries', transform material substances? But this was so to a far higher degree of traders and merchants, who partook in a network wholly outside the perception and understanding of ordinary people. They engaged in something like the transformation of the non-material in altering the value of goods. How could the power of things to satisfy human needs change without a change in their quantity? The trader or merchant, the one who seemed to effect such changes, standing outside the seen, agreed and understood order of daily affairs, also was thrust outside the established hierarchy of status and respect. So it was that traders were held in contempt even by Plato and Aristotle, citizens of a city which in their day owed her leading position to trade. Later, under feudal conditions, commercial pursuits continued to be held in relatively low esteem, for traders and craftsmen, at least outside a few small towns, then depended for security of life and limb, as well as of goods, on those who wielded the sword and, with it, protected the roads. Trade could develop only under the protection of a class whose profession was arms, whose members depended on their physical prowess, and who claimed in return high status and a high standard of life. Such attitudes, even when conditions began to change, tended to linger wherever feudalism persisted, or was unopposed by a wealthy bourgeoisie or trading centres in self-governing towns. Thus, even as late as the end of the last century, we are told of

Japan that 'the makers of money were almost a class of untouchables'.

The ostracism of traders becomes even more understandable when it is remembered that merchant activity is indeed often cloaked in mystery. 'The mysteries of the trades' meant that some gained from knowledge that others lacked, a knowledge the more mysterious in that it often dealt with foreign – and perhaps even disgusting – customs, as well as unknown lands: lands of legend and rumour. 'Ex nihilo nihil fit' may no longer be part of science (see Popper, 1977/84:14; and Bartley, 1978:675–76), but it still dominates common sense. Activities that appear to add to available wealth, 'out of nothing', without physical creation and by merely rearranging what already exists, stink of sorcery.

A neglected influence reinforcing such prejudices has to do with physical effort, muscular activity, and the 'sweat of one's brows'. Physical strength, and the ordinary tools and weapons that often accompany its employment, are not only observable but tangible. There is nothing mysterious about them, even for most people who lack them themselves. The conviction that physical effort, and the capacity for it, are in themselves meritorious and confer rank hardly had to wait for feudal times. It was part of the inherited instinct of the small group, and was preserved among farmers, tillers of the soil, herdsmen, warriors, and even simple householders and handicraftsmen. People could see how the physical effort of the farmer or artisan added to the total of visible useful things – and account for differences of wealth and power in terms of recognisable causes.

Thus physical competition was introduced and appreciated early, as primitive man became familiar, both in competition for leadership and in games of skill (see Appendix E), with ways of testing visible superiority of strength. But as soon as knowledge – which was not 'open' or visible – was introduced as an element in competition, knowledge not possessed by other participants, and which must have seemed to many of them also to be beyond the possibility of possession, the familiarity and sense of fairness vanished. Such competition threatened solidarity and the pursuit of agreed purposes. Viewed from the perspective of the extended order, of course, such a reaction must appear quite selfish, or perhaps as a curious kind of group egotism in which the solidarity of the group outweighs the welfare of its individuals.

Such sentiment was still vigorous in the nineteenth century. Thus, when Thomas Carlyle, who had great influence among the literati of the last century, preached that 'work alone is noble' (1909:160), he explicitly meant physical, even muscular, effort. To him, as to Karl Marx, labour was the real source of wealth. This particular sentiment may today be waning. Indeed, the connection of productivity with human physical prowess, though still valued by our instincts, plays an ever smaller role in human endeavour, wherein power now less often means physical might as legal right. Of course we can still not do without some very strong individuals, but they are becoming merely one kind of an increasing number of ever smaller groups of specialists. Only among primitives do the physically strong still dominate.

However this may be, activities such as barter and exchange and more elaborate forms of trade, the organisation or direction of activities, and the shifting about of available goods for sale in accordance with profitability, are still not always even regarded as *real work*. It remains hard for many to accept that quantitative increases of available supplies of physical means of subsistence and enjoyment should depend less on the visible transformation of physical substances into other physical substances than on the shifting about of objects which thereby change their relevant magnitudes and values. That is, the market process deals with material objects, but its shifting around of them does not seem to add (whatever might be claimed or really be so) to their perceptible quantities. The market transmits information about them rather than producing them, and the crucial function played by the conveying of information escapes the notice of persons guided by mechanistic or scientistic habits who take for granted factual information about physical objects and disregard the role played, in the determination of value, by the relative scarcity of different kinds of objects.

There is an irony here: that precisely those who do not think of economic events in literally materialistic terms – that is, in terms of physical quantities of material substances – but are guided by calculations in terms of value, i.e., by the appreciation that men have for these objects, and particularly those differences between costs and price that are called profits, should habitually be denounced as materialists. Whereas it is precisely the striving for profit that makes it possible for those engaged in it not to think in terms of material quantities of particular concrete needs of known individuals, but of the best way in which they can contribute to an aggregate output that results from the similar separate efforts of countless unknown others.

There is also an error in economics here – an idea that even Carl Menger's brother Anton propagated, the notion that the 'whole product of labour' stems mainly from physical effort; and although this is an old mistake, it is probably John Stuart Mill as much as anyone who is responsible for spreading it. Mill wrote in his *Principles of Political Economy* (1848, 'Of Property', Book II, ch. I, sect. 1; *Works*, II:260) that while 'the laws and the conditions of the production of wealth partake of the character of physical truths', distribution is 'a matter of human institutions only. The things once there, mankind individually or collectively can do with them as

92

they like', from which he concluded that 'society can subject this distribution of wealth to whatever rules it can think out'. Mill, who is here considering the size of the product as a purely technological problem, independent of its distribution, overlooks the dependence of size on the *use* made of existing opportunities, which is an economic and not a technological problem. We owe it to methods of 'distribution', that is, to the determination of prices, that the product is as large as it is. What there is to share depends on the principle by which production is organised – that is, in a market economy, on pricing and distribution. It is simply wrong to conclude that 'the things once there', we are free to do with them as we like, *for they will not be there* unless individuals have generated price information by securing for themselves certain shares of the total.

There is a further error. Like Marx, Mill treated market values exclusively as effects and not also as causes of human decisions. We shall see later, when we turn to discuss marginal utility theory explicitly, how inaccurate this is – and how wrong was Mill's declaration that 'there is nothing in the laws of value which remains for the present or any future writer to clear up; the theory of the subject is complete' (1848:III, I, sect. 1, in *Works*, II:199–200).

Trade – regarded as real work or not – brought not only individual but also collective wealth through effort of brain rather than of muscles. That a mere change of hands should lead to a gain in value to all participants, that it need not mean gain to one at the expense of the others (or what has come to be called exploitation), was and is nonetheless intuitively difficult to grasp. The example of Henry Ford is sometimes brought forward to allay suspicions, to illustrate how striving for profit benefits the masses. The example is indeed illuminating because in it one does easily see how an entrepreneur could directly aim at satisfying an observable need of large numbers of people, and how his efforts did in fact succeed in raising their standard of living. But the example is also insufficient; for in most cases the effects of increases of productivity are too indirect to trace them so plainly. An improvement in, say, the production of metal screws, or string, or window glass, or paper, would spread its benefits so widely that far less concrete perception of causes and effects would remain.

As a consequence of all these circumstances, many people continue to find the mental feats associated with trade easy to discount even when they do not attribute them to sorcery, or see them as depending on trick or fraud or cunning deceit. Wealth so obtained appeared even less related to any visible desert (i.e., desert dependent on physical exertion) than did the luck of the hunter or fisher.

But if wealth generated by such 'rearrangements' bewildered folk, the information-searching activities of tradesmen evoked truly great distrust. The transport involved in trade can usually be at least partly understood by the layman, at least after some patient explanation and argument, to be productive. For example, the view that trade only shifts about already existing things can be readily corrected by pointing out that many things can be made only by assembling substances from widely distant places. The relative value of these substances will depend not on the attributes of the individual material components of which they consist but on relative quantities available *together* at the locations required. Thus trade in raw materials and semi-finished products is a precondition for increase in the physical quantities of many final products that could only be manufactured at all thanks to the availability of (perhaps small quantities of) materials fetched from far away. The quantity of a particular product that can be produced from resources found at a particular place may depend on the availability of a very much smaller quantity of another substance (such as mercury or phosphor, or perhaps even a catalyst) that can be obtained only at the other end of the earth. Trade thus creates the very possibility of physical production.

The idea that such productivity, and even such bringing together of supplies, also depends on a continuous successful search for widely dispersed and constantly changing information remains harder to grasp, however obvious it may seem to those who have understood the process by which trade creates and guides physical production when steered by information about the relative scarcity of different things at different places.

Perhaps the main force behind the persistent dislike of commercial dealings is then no more than plain ignorance and conceptual difficulty. This is however compounded with preexisting fear of the unfamiliar: a fear of sorcery and the unnatural, and also a fear of knowledge itself harking back to our origins and indelibly memorialised in the first few chapters of the book of Genesis, in the story of man's expulsion from the Garden of Eden. All superstitions, including socialism, feed on such fear.

Marginal Utility versus Macro-economics

The fear may be powerful, but it is unfounded. Such activities are of course not *really* incomprehensible. Economics and the biological sciences, as we have seen in the foregoing chapters, now give a good account of self-organising processes, and we have sketched a partial rational reconstruction of some of their history and beneficial effects in the rise and spread of civilisation in chapters two and three above (see also Hayek, 1973).

Exchange is productive; it does increase the satisfaction of human needs from available resources. Civilisation is so complex – and trade so productive – because the subjective worlds of the individuals living in the civilised world differ so much. Apparently paradoxically, diversity of individual purposes leads to a greater power to satisfy needs generally than does homogeneity, unanimity and control – and, also paradoxically, this is so because diversity enables men to master and dispose of *more* information. Only a clear analysis of the market process can resolve these apparent paradoxes.

An increase of value – crucial in exchange and trade – is indeed different from increases in quantity observable by our senses. Increase in value is something for which laws governing physical events, at least as understood within materialist and mechanistic models, do not account. Value indicates the potential capacities of an object or action to satisfy human needs, and can be ascertained only by the mutual adjustment through exchange of the respective (marginal) rates of substitution (or equivalence) which different goods or services have for various individuals. Value is not an attribute or physical property possessed by things themselves, irrespective of their relations to men, but solely an aspect of these relations that enables men to take account, in their decisions about the use of such things, of the better opportunities others might have for their use. Increase in value appears only with, and is relevant only with regard to, human purposes. As Carl Menger made clear (1871/1981:121), value 'is a judgement economising men make about the importance of goods at their disposal for the maintenance of their lives and well-being'. Economic value expresses changing degrees of the capacity of things to satisfy some of the multiplicity of separate, individual scales of ends.

Each person has his own peculiar order for ranking the ends that he pursues. These individual rankings can be known to few, if any, others, and are hardly known fully even by the person himself. The efforts of millions of individuals in different situations, with different possessions and desires, having access to different information about means, knowing little or nothing about one another's particular needs, and aiming at different scales of ends, are coordinated by means of exchange systems. As individuals reciprocally align with one another, an undesigned system of a higher order of complexity comes into being, and a continuous flow of goods and services is created that, for a remarkably high number of the participating individuals, fulfils their guiding expectations and values.

The multiplicity of different ranks of different ends produces a common, and uniform, scale of intermediate or reflected values of the material means for which these ends compete. Since most material means can be used for many different ends of varying importance, and diverse means can often be substituted for one another, the ultimate values of the ends come to be reflected in a single scale of values of means – i.e., prices – that depends on their relative scarcity and the possibility of exchange among their owners.

Since changing factual circumstances require constant adaptation of particular ends to whose service particular kinds of means must be assigned, the two sets of scales of value are bound to change in different manners and at different rates. The several orders of ranking of individual ultimate ends, while different, will show a certain stability, but the relative values of the means toward whose production those individuals' efforts are directed will be subject to continuous fortuitous fluctuations that cannot be anticipated and whose causes will be unintelligible to most people.

That the hierarchy of ends is relatively stable (reflecting what many may regard as their constant or 'lasting' value), whereas the hierarchy of means fluctuates so much, leads many idealistic persons to prize the former and disdain the latter. To serve a constantly changing scale of values may indeed seem repulsive. This is perhaps the fundamental reason why those most concerned about ultimate ends nonetheless often, contrary to their own objectives, attempt to thwart the procedure by which they can best contribute to their realisation. Most people must, to achieve their own ends, pursue what are merely means for themselves as well as for others. That is, they must engage at some point in a long chain of activities which will eventually lead to the satisfaction of an unknown need at some remote time and place, after passing through many intermediate stages directed to different ends. The label which the market process attaches to the immediate product is all the individual can know in most instances. No person engaged in some stage of the process of making metallic screws, for instance, can possibly rationally determine when, where, or how the particular piece on which he is working will or ought to contribute to the satisfaction of human needs. Nor do statistics help him to decide which of many potential uses to which it (or any other similar item) could be put, should be satisfied, and which not.

But also contributing to the feeling that the scale of values of means, i.e., prices, is common or vulgar, is apparently that it is the same for all, while different scales of ends are distinctive and personal. We prove our individuality by asserting our particular tastes or by showing our more discriminating appreciation of quality. Yet only because of information, through prices, about the relative scarcity of different means are we able to realise as many of our ends as we do.

The apparent conflict between the two kinds of hierarchies of values

96

becomes conspicuous in the extended order, in which most people earn their living by providing means for others unknown to them, and equally obtain the means they require for their own purposes from still others also unknown to them. The only common scales of values thus become those of means, whose importance does not chiefly depend on effects perceived by those who use a particular item but are readily substituable for one another. Owing to demands for a great variety of ends by a multiplicity of individuals, the concrete uses for which a particular thing is wanted by others (and therefore the value each will put on it) will not be known. This abstract character of the merely instrumental value of means also contributes to the disdain for what is felt to be the 'artificial' or 'unnatural' character of their value.

Adequate explanations of such puzzling and even alarming phenomena, first discovered scarcely a hundred years ago, were disseminated as the work of William Stanley Jevons, Carl Menger, and Léon Walras was developed, especially by the Austrian school following Menger, into what became known as the 'subjective' or 'marginal utility' revolution in economic theory. If what has been said in the preceding paragraphs sounds unfamiliar as well as difficult, this suggests that the most elementary and important discoveries of this revolution have even now not reached general awareness. It was the discovery that economic events could not be explained by preceding events acting as determining causes that enabled these revolutionary thinkers to unify economic theory into a coherent system. Although classical economics, or what is often called 'classical political economy', had already provided an analysis of the process of competition, and particularly of the manner in which international trade integrated national orders of cooperation into an international one, only marginal utility theory brought real understanding of how demand and supply were determined, of how quantities were adapted to needs, and of how measures of scarcity resulting from mutual adjustment guided individuals. The whole market process then became understood as a process of transfer of information enabling men to use, and put to work, much more information and skill than they would have access to individually.

That the utility of an object or action, usually defined as its capacity to satisfy human wants, is not of the same magnitude to different individuals, now seems so obvious that it is difficult to understand how serious scientists should ever have treated utility as an objective, general and even measurable attribute of physical objects. That the relative utilities of different objects to different persons can be distinguished does not provide the least basis for comparisons of their absolute magnitude. Nor, although people may agree how much they are

97

individually prepared to contribute to the costs of different utilities, does 'collective utility' denote a discoverable object: it exists as little as a collective mind, and is at best a metaphor. Nor does the fact that we all occasionally decide that some object is more or less important to another person than to ourselves provide any reason to believe in objective interpersonal comparison of utility.

Indeed, in a certain sense the activity that economics sets out to explain is not *about* physical phenomena but about people. Economic values are interpretations of physical facts in the light of the degrees of suitability of kinds of physical objects in particular situations for the satisfaction of needs. Thus one might describe economics (what I now prefer to call catallactics (Hayek, 1973)) as a *meta*theory, a *theory about* the theories people have developed to explain how most effectively to discover and use different means for diverse purposes. Under the circumstances it is not so surprising that physical scientists, on encountering such arguments, often find themselves in strange territory, or that such economists often strike them more like philosophers than 'real' scientists.

Marginal utility theory is, although a basic advance, one that has been obscured from the start. The most accessible early statement of the idea in the English-speaking world, by W. S. Jevons, remained after his early death, and also in consequence of the extra-academic position of his single eminent follower, Wicksteed, long disregarded due to the dominant academic authority of Alfred Marshall, who was reluctant to depart from the position of John Stuart Mill. The Austrian co-discoverer of the theory, Carl Menger, was more fortunate in finding at once two highly gifted pupils (Eugen von Böhm–Bawerk and Friedrich von Wieser) to continue his work and to establish a tradition, with the result that modern economic theory gradually came to be generally accepted under the name of the 'Austrian School'. By its stress on what it called the 'subjective' nature of economic values it produced a new paradigm for explaining structures arising without design from human interaction. Yet, during the last forty years, its contributions have been obscured by the rise of 'macro-economics', which seeks causal connections between hypothetically measurable entities or statistical aggregates. These may sometimes, I concede, indicate some *vague* probabilities, but they certainly do not explain the processes involved in generating them.

But because of the delusion that macro-economics is both viable and useful (a delusion encouraged by its extensive use of mathematics, which must always impress politicians lacking any mathematical education, and which is really the nearest thing to the practice of magic that occurs among professional economists) many opinions ruling contemporary government and politics are still based on naive explanations of such economic phenomena as value and prices, explanations that vainly endeavour to account for them as 'objective' occurrences independent of human knowledge and aims. Such explanations cannot interpret the function or appreciate the indispensability of trading and markets for coordinating the productive efforts of large numbers of people.

> Some habits that have crept into mathematical analysis of the market process often mislead even trained economists. For example, the practice of referring to 'the existing state of knowledge', and to information available to acting members of a market process either as 'data' or as 'given' (or even by the pleonasm of 'given data'), often leads economists to assume that this knowledge exists not merely in dispersed form but that the whole of it might be available to some single mind. This conceals the character of competition as a discovery procedure. What in these treatments of the market order is represented as a 'problem' to be solved is not really a problem to anyone in the market, since the determining factual circumstances on which the market in such an order depends cannot be known to anyone, and the problem is not how to use *given* knowledge available as a whole, but how to make it possible that knowledge which is not, and cannot be, made available to any one mind, can yet be used, in its fragmentary and dispersed form, by many interacting individuals – a problem not for the actors but for the theoreticians trying to explain those actions.

The creation of wealth is not simply a physical process and cannot be explained by a chain of cause and effect. It is determined not by objective physical facts known to any one mind but by the separate, differing, information of millions, which is precipitated in prices that serve to guide further decisions. When the market tells an individual entrepreneur that more profit is to be gained in a particular way, he can both serve his own advantage and also make a larger contribution to the aggregate (in terms of the same units of calculation that most others use) than he could produce in any other available way. For these prices inform market participants of crucial momentary conditions on which the whole division of labour depends: the actual rate of convertibility (or 'substitutability') of different resources for one another, whether as means to produce other goods or to satisfy particular human needs. For this it is even irrelevant what quantities are available to mankind as a whole. Such 'macro-economic' knowledge of aggregate quantities available of different things is neither available nor needed, nor would it even be useful. Any idea of measuring the aggregate product composed of a great variety of commodities in varying combinations is mistaken:

99

their equivalence for human purposes depends on human knowledge, and only after we have translated physical quantities into economic values can we begin to estimate such matters.

What is decisive for the magnitude of the product, and the chief determinant generating particular quantities, is how those millions of individuals who have distinctive knowledge of particular resources combine them at various places and times into assemblies, choosing among the great varieties of possibilities – none of which possibilities can by itself be called the most effective without knowing the relative scarcity of different elements as indicated by their prices.

> The decisive step towards understanding the role of relative prices in determining the best use of resources was Ricardo's discovery of the principle of comparative costs, of which Ludwig von Mises rightly said that it ought to be called the Ricardian Law of Association (1949:159–64). Price relations alone tell the entrepreneur where return sufficiently exceeds costs to make it profitable to devote limited capital to a particular undertaking. Such signs direct him to an invisible goal, the satisfaction of the distant unknown consumer of the final product.

The Intellectuals' Economic Ignorance

An understanding of trade and of marginal-utility explanations of the determination of relative values is crucial for comprehending the order on which the nourishment of the existing multitudes of human beings depends. Such matters ought to be familiar to every educated person. Such understanding has been thwarted by the general disdain with which intellectuals tend to treat the entire subject. For the fact made clear by marginal utility theory – namely, that it could become every individual's distinct task, by his several knowledge and skills, to help satisfy the needs of the community through a contribution *of his choice* – is equally foreign to the primitive mind and to the reigning constructivism, as well as to explicit socialism.

It is no exaggeration to say that this notion marks the emancipation of the individual. To the development of the individualist spirit are due (see chapters two and three above) the division of skills, knowledge and labour on which advanced civilisation rests. As contemporary economic historians like Braudel (1981–84) have begun to comprehend, the disdained middleman, striving for gain, made possible the modern extended order, modern technology, and the magnitude of our current population. The ability, no less than the freedom, to be guided by one's own knowledge and decisions, rather than being carried away by the spirit of the group, are developments of the intellect which our emotions have followed only imperfectly. Here again, although members of a primitive group may readily concede superior knowledge to a revered leader, they resent it in the fellow who knows a way to obtain by little perceptible effort what others can get only by hard work. To conceal and to use superior information for individual or private gain is still regarded as somehow improper – or at least unneighbourly. And these primitive reactions remain active long after specialisation has become the only way to make use of the acquisition of information in its great variety.

Such reactions also continue today to influence political opinion and action, to thwart the development of the most effective organisation of production, and to encourage the false hopes of socialism. That mankind – which owes the supplies on which it lives as much to trade as to production – should despise the first but overly esteem the second creates a state of affairs that cannot help but have a distorting effect on political attitudes.

Ignorance of the function of trade, which led initially to fear, and in the Middle Ages to uninformed regulation, and which only comparatively recently yielded to better understanding, has, then, now been revived in a new pseudo-scientific form. In this form it lends itself to attempts at technocratic economic manipulation which, when they inevitably fail, encourage a modern form of distrust of 'capitalism'. Yet the situation may seem worse still when we turn our attention to certain further ordering processes, even harder to understand than is trade, i.e., those governing money and finance.

The Distrust of Money and Finance

Prejudice arising from the distrust of the mysterious reaches an even higher pitch when directed at those most abstract institutions of an advanced civilisation on which trade depends, which mediate the most general, indirect, remote and unperceived effects of individual action, and which, though indispensable for the formation of an extended order, tend to veil their guiding mechanisms from probing observation: money and the financial institutions based on it. The moment that barter is replaced by indirect exchange mediated by money, ready intelligibility ceases and abstract interpersonal processes begin that far transcend even the most enlightened individual perception.

Money, the very 'coin' of ordinary interaction, is hence of all things the least understood and – perhaps with sex – the object of greatest unreasoning fantasy; and like sex it simultaneously fascinates, puzzles and repels. The literature treating it is probably greater than that devoted to any other single subject; and browsing through it inclines one to sympathise with the writer who long ago declared that no other

101

subject, not even love, has driven more men to madness. 'The love of money', the Bible declares, 'is the root of all evil' (*I Timothy*, 6:10). But *ambivalence* about it is perhaps even more common: money appears as at once the most powerful instrument of freedom and the most sinister tool of oppression. This most widely-accepted medium of exchange conjures up all the unease that people feel towards a process they cannot understand, that they both love and hate, and some of whose effects they desire passionately while detesting others that are inseparable from the first.

The operation of the money and credit structure has, however, with language and morals, been one of the spontaneous orders most resistant to efforts at adequate theoretical explanation, and it remains the object of serious disagreement among specialists. Even some professional students have resigned themselves to the insight that the particulars necessarily escape perception, and that the complexity of the whole compels one to be content with accounts of abstract patterns that form themselves spontaneously, accounts which, however enlightening, give no power to predict any particular result.

Money and finance trouble not only the student. Like trade and for many of the same reasons, they remain unremittingly suspect to moralists. The moralist has several reasons for distrusting this universal means of obtaining and manipulating power over the greatest variety of ends in the least visible manner. First, whereas one could readily see how many other objects of wealth were used, the concrete or particular effects of the use of money on oneself or on other people often remain indiscernible. Second, even when some of its effects are discernible, it may be used for good and bad ends alike – hence the supreme versatility that makes it so useful to its possessor also makes it the more suspect to the moralist. Finally, its skilful use, and the large gains and magnitudes arising from it, appear, as with commerce, divorced from physical effort or recognisable merit, and need not even be concerned with any material substrate – as in 'purely paper transactions'. If craftsmen and blacksmiths were feared for transforming material substance, if traders were feared for transforming such intangible qualities as value, how much more will the banker be feared for the transformations he effects with the most abstract and immaterial of all economic institutions? Thus we reach the climax of the progressive replacement of the perceivable and concrete by abstract concepts shaping rules guiding activity: money and its institutions seem to lie beyond the boundary of laudable and understandable physical efforts of creation, in a realm where the comprehension of the concrete ceases and incomprehensible abstractions rule.

Thus the subject at once bewilders specialists and offends moralists:

both are alarmed to find that the whole has outgrown our capacity to survey or control the sequence of events on which we depend. It seems all to have got out of hand, or as the German expression more tellingly puts it, *ist uns über den Kopf gewachsen*. No wonder the expressions that refer to money are so emphatic, even hyperbolic. Perhaps some still believe, as Cicero (*De officiis*, II:89) tells us of the elder Cato, that money-lending is as bad as murder. Although the Roman followers of the Stoics, such as Cicero himself and Seneca, did show more understanding of such matters, current views about market-determined rates of interest on loans are hardly more flattering, even though the latter are so important in directing capital to its most productive uses. Thus we still hear of the 'cash nexus', 'filthy lucre', 'the acquisitive instinct', and the activities of the 'huckster' (for an account of all this see Braudel, 1982b).

Nor do the problems end with the expression of rude epithets. Like morality, law, language, and biological organisms, monetary institutions result from spontaneous order – and are similarly susceptible to variation and selection. Yet monetary institutions turn out to be the least satisfactorily developed of all spontaneously grown formations. Few will, for example, dare to claim that their functioning has improved during the last seventy years or so, since what had been an essentially automatic mechanism based on an international metallic standard was replaced, under the guidance of experts, by deliberate national 'monetary policies'. Indeed, humankind's experiences with money have given good reason for distrusting it, but not for the reasons commonly supposed. *Rather, the selective processes are interfered with here more than anywhere else: selection by evolution is prevented by government monopolies that make competitive experimentation impossible.*

Under government patronage the monetary system has grown to great complexity, but so little private experimentation and selection among alternative means has ever been permitted that we still do not quite know what good money would be – or how good it could be. Nor is such interference and monopoly a recent creation: it occurred almost as soon as coinage was adopted as a generally accepted medium of exchange. Though an indispensable requirement for the functioning of an extensive order of cooperation of free people, money has almost from its first appearance been so shamelessly abused by governments that it has become the prime source of disturbance of all self-ordering processes in the extended order of human cooperation. The history of government management of money has, except for a few short happy periods, been one of incessant fraud and deception. In this respect, governments have proved far more immoral than any private agency supplying distinct kinds of money in competition possibly could have been. I have suggested elsewhere, and will not argue again here, that the market economy might well be better able to develop its potentialities if government monopoly of money were abolished (Hayek, 1976/78, and 1986:8–10).

However this may be, our main subject here, the persistent adverse opinion of 'pecuniary considerations', is based on ignorance of the indispensable role money plays in making possible the extended order of human cooperation and general calculation in market values. Money is indispensable for extending reciprocal cooperation beyond the limits of human awareness – and therefore also beyond the limits of what was explicable and could be readily recognised as expanding opportunities.

The Condemnation of Profit and the Contempt for Trade

The objections of the *beaux esprits* of our own time – those intellectuals we have just mentioned again, and with whom we were concerned in earlier chapters – do not differ so very much from the objections of members of primitive groups; and it is this that has inclined me to call their demands and longings atavistic. What intellectuals steeped in constructivist presuppositions find most objectionable in the market order, in trade, in money and the institutions of finance, is that producers, traders, and financiers are not concerned with concrete needs of known people but with abstract calculation of costs and profit. But they forget, or have not learned, the arguments that we have just rehearsed. Concern for profit is just what makes possible the more effective use of resources. It makes the most productive use of the variety of potential support that can be enlisted from other business undertakings. The high-minded socialist slogan, 'Production for use, not for profit', which we find in one form or another from Aristotle to Bertrand Russell, from Albert Einstein to Archbishop Camara of Brazil (and often, since Aristotle, with the addition that these profits are made 'at the expense of others'), betrays ignorance of how productive capacity is multiplied by different individuals obtaining access to different knowledge whose total exceeds what any single one of them could muster. The entrepreneur *must* in his activities probe beyond known uses and ends if he is to provide means for producing yet other means which in turn serve still others, and so on – that is, if he is to serve a *multiplicity* of ultimate ends. Prices and profit are all that most producers need to be able to serve more effectively the needs of men they do not know. They are a tool for searching – just as, for the soldier or hunter, the seaman or air pilot, the telescope extends the range of vision. The market process gives most people the material and information resources that they need in order to obtain *what they want*. Hence few things are more irresponsible than the derision of concern with costs by intellectuals who, commonly, do not know how to go about finding out how particular results are to be achieved at the least sacrifice of other ends. These intellectuals are blinded by indignation about that essential *chance* of very large gains that seem disproportionate to the effort required in a particular case, but that alone makes this kind of experimentation practicable.

It is hence hard to believe that anyone accurately informed about the market can honestly condemn the search for profit. The disdain of profit is due to ignorance, and to an attitude that we may if we wish admire in the ascetic who has chosen to be content with a small share of the riches of this world, but which, when actualised in the form of restrictions on profits of others, is selfish to the extent that it imposes asceticism, and indeed deprivations of all sorts, on others.

SEVEN

OUR POISONED LANGUAGE

When words lose their meaning
people will lose their liberty.

Confucius

Words as Guides to Action

Trade, migration, and the increase and mixture of populations must not only have opened people's eyes, but also loosened their tongues. It was not simply that tradesmen inevitably encountered, and sometimes mastered, foreign languages during their travels, but that this must have forced them also to ponder the different connotations of key words (if only to avoid either affronting their hosts or misunderstanding the terms of agreements to exchange), and thereby to come to know new and different views about the most basic matters. I should like now to consider some of the problems relating to language that attend the conflict between the primitive group and the extended order.

All people, whether primitive or civilised, organise what they perceive partly by means of attributes that language has taught them to attach to groups of sensory characteristics. Language enables us not only to label objects given to our senses as distinct entities, but also to classify an infinite variety of combinations of distinguishing marks according to what we expect from them and what we may do with them. Such labelling, classification, and distinction is of course often vague. More importantly, all usage of language is laden with interpretations or theories about our surroundings. As Goethe recognised, all that we imagine to be factual is already theory: what we 'know' of our surroundings is our interpretation of them.

As a consequence, various difficulties arise in analysing and criticising our own views. For example, many widely held beliefs live only implicitly in words or phrases implying them and may never become explicit; thus they are never exposed to the possibility of criticism, with the result that language transmits not only wisdom but also a type of folly that is difficult to eradicate.

It is also difficult to explain in a particular vocabulary – because of its own limitations and because of the connotations it bears – something that differs from what that language had traditionally been used to explain. Not only is it difficult to explain, or even to describe something new in received terms, it also may be hard to sort out what language has previously classified in a particular manner – especially a manner based on innate distinctions of our senses.

Such difficulties have driven some scientists to invent new languages for their own disciplines. Reformers, and especially socialists, have been driven by the same urge, and some of them have proposed deliberate reformation of language in order the better to convert people to their own position (see Bloch, 1954–59).

In view of such difficulties, our vocabulary, and the theories embedded in it, are crucial. So long as we speak in language based in erroneous theory, we generate and perpetuate error. Yet the traditional vocabulary that still profoundly shapes our perception of the world and of human interaction within it – and the theories and interpretations embedded in that vocabulary – remain in many ways very primitive. Much of it was formed during long past epochs in which our minds interpreted very differently what our senses conveyed. Thus, while we learn much of what we know through language, the meanings of individual words lead us astray: we continue to use terms bearing archaic connotations as we try to express our new and better understanding of the phenomena to which they refer.

A pertinent example is the way transitive verbs ascribe to inanimate objects some sort of mind-like action. Just as the naive or untutored mind tends to assume the presence of life wherever it perceives movement, it also tends to assume the activity of mind or spirit wherever it imagines that there is purpose. The situation is aggravated by the fact that, to some degree, the evolution of the human race seems to repeat itself during the early development of each human mind. In his account of *The Child's Conception of the World* (1929:359), Jean Piaget writes: 'The child begins by seeing purpose everywhere.' Only secondarily is the mind concerned with differentiating between purposes of the things themselves (animism) and purposes of the makers of the things (artificialism). Animistic connotations cling to many basic words, and particularly to those describing occurrences producing order. Not only 'fact' itself but also 'to cause', 'coerce', 'distribute', 'prefer', and 'organise', terms indispensable in the description of impersonal processes, still evoke in many minds the idea of a personal actor.

The word 'order' itself is a clear instance of an expression which, before Darwin, would have been taken almost universally to imply a personal actor. At the beginning of the last century even a thinker of the stature of Jeremy Bentham maintained that 'order presupposes an end' (1789/1887, *Works*:II, 399). Indeed, it could be said that, until the

107

'subjective revolution' in economic theory of the 1870's, understanding of human creation was dominated by animism – a conception from which even Adam Smith's 'invisible hand' provided only a partial escape until, in the 1870's, the guide-role of competitively-determined market prices came to be more clearly understood. Yet even now, outside the scientific examination of law, language and the market, studies of human affairs continue to be dominated by a vocabulary chiefly derived from animistic thinking.

One of the most important examples comes from socialist writers. The more closely one scrutinises their work, the more clearly one sees that they have contributed far more to the preservation than to the reformation of animistic thought and language. Take for instance the personification of 'society' in the historicist tradition of Hegel, Comte and Marx. Socialism, with its 'society', is indeed the latest form of those animistic interpretations of order historically represented by various religions (with their 'gods'). The fact that socialism is often directed against religion hardly mitigates this point. Imagining that all order is the result of design, socialists conclude that order must be improvable by better design of some superior mind. For this socialism deserves a place in an authoritative inventory of the various forms of animism – such as that given, in a preliminary way, by E. E. Evans–Pritchard in his *Theories of Primitive Religion* (1965). In view of the continuing influence of such animism, it seems premature even today to agree with W. K. Clifford, a profound thinker who, already during Darwin's lifetime, asserted that '*purpose* has ceased to suggest *design* to instructed people except in cases where the agency of men is independently probable' (1879:117).

The continuing influence of socialism on the language of intellectuals and scholars is evident also in descriptive studies of history and anthropology. As Braudel asks: 'Who among us has not spoken about the *class struggle*, the *modes of production*, the *labour force*, the *surplus value*, the *relative pauperisation*, the *practice*, the *alienation*, the *infrastructure*, the *superstructure*, the *use value*, the *exchange value*, the *primitive accumulation*, the *dialectics*, the *dictatorship of the proletariat* . . .?' (supposedly all derived from or popularised by Karl Marx: see Braudel 1982b).

In most instances, underlying this sort of talk are not simple statements of fact but interpretations or theories about consequences or causes of alleged facts. To Marx especially we also owe the substitution of the term 'society' for the state or compulsory organisation about which he is really talking, a circumlocution that suggests that we can deliberately regulate the actions of individuals by some gentler and kinder method of direction than coercion. Of course the extended, spontaneous order that has been the main subject matter of this volume

108

would have been as little able to 'act' or to 'treat' particular persons as would a people or a population. On the other hand, the 'state' or, better, the 'government', which before Hegel used to be the common (and more honest) English word, evidently connoted for Marx too openly and clearly the idea of authority while the vague term 'society' allowed him to insinuate that its rule would secure some sort of freedom.

Thus, while wisdom is often hidden in the meaning of words, so is error. Naive interpretations that we now know to be false, as well as profoundly helpful if often unappreciated advice, survive and determine our decisions through the words we use. Of particular relevance to our discussion is the unfortunate fact that many words that we apply to various aspects of the extended order of human cooperation carry misleading connotations of an earlier kind of community. Indeed, many words embodied in our language are of such a character that, if one habitually employs them, one is led to conclusions not implied by any sober thought about the subject in question, conclusions that also conflict with scientific evidence. It was for this reason that in writing this book I imposed upon myself the self-denying ordinance never to use the words 'society' or 'social' (though they unavoidably occur occasionally in titles of books and in quotations I draw from statements of others; and I have also, on a few occasions, let the expressions 'the social sciences' or 'social studies' stand). Yet, while I have not hitherto *used* these terms, in this chapter I wish to *discuss* them – as well as some other words that function similarly – to expose some of the poison concealed in our language, particularly in that language which concerns the orders and structures of human interaction and interrelationship.

The somewhat simplified quotation by Confucius that stands at the head of this chapter is probably the earliest expression of this concern that has been preserved. An abbreviated form in which I first encountered it apparently stems from there being in Chinese no single word (or set of characters) for liberty. It would also appear, however, that the passage legitimately renders Confucius's account of the desirable condition of any ordered group of men, as expressed in his *Analects* (tr. A. Waley, 1938:XIII, 3, 171–2): 'If the language is incorrect . . . the people will have nowhere to put hand and foot'. I am obliged to David Hawkes, of Oxford, for having traced a truer rendering of a passage I had often quoted in an incorrect form.

The unsatisfactory character of our contemporary vocabulary of political terms results from its descent largely from Plato and Aristotle who, lacking the conception of evolution, considered the order of human affairs as an arrangement of a fixed and unchanging number of men fully known to the governing authority – or, like most religions down to socialism, as the designed product of some superior mind. (Anyone who wishes to pursue the influence of words on political thinking will find rich information in Demandt (1978). In English a helpful discussion of the deceptions brought on by metaphorical language will be found in Cohen (1931); but the fullest discussions of the political abuse of language known to me occur in the German studies of Schoeck (1973), and in H. Schelsky (1975:233–249). I have myself treated some of these matters earlier in my (1967/78:71–97; 1973:26–54; 1976:78–80).)

Terminological Ambiguity and Distinctions among Systems of Coordination

Elsewhere we have tried to disentangle some of the confusions caused by the ambiguity of terms such as 'natural' and 'artificial' (see Appendix A), of 'genetic' and 'cultural' and the like, and as the reader will have noticed, I generally prefer the less usual but more precise term 'several property' to the more common expression 'private property'. There are of course many other ambiguities and confusions, some of them of greater importance.

For instance, there was the deliberate deception practiced by American socialists in their appropriation of the term 'liberalism'. As Joseph A. Schumpeter rightly put it (1954:394): 'As a supreme if unintended compliment, the enemies of the system of private enterprise have thought it wise to appropriate its label.' The same applies increasingly to European political parties of the middle, which either, as in Britain, carry the name liberal or, as in West Germany, claim to be liberal but do not hesitate to form coalitions with openly socialist parties. It has, as I complained over twenty-five years ago (1960, Postscript), become almost impossible for a Gladstonian liberal to describe himself as a liberal without giving the impression that he believes in socialism. Nor is this a new development: as long ago as 1911, L. T. Hobhouse published a book under the title *Liberalism* that would more correctly have been called *Socialism*, promptly followed by a book entitled *The Elements of Social Justice* (1922).

Important as is this particular change – one perhaps now beyond remedying – we must concentrate here, in accordance with the general theme of this book, on the ambiguities and vagueness caused by the names generally given to phenomena of human interaction. The inadequacy of the terms we use to refer to different forms of human interaction is just one more symptom, one more manifestation, of the prevailing, highly inadequate intellectual grasp of the processes by which human efforts are coordinated. These terms are indeed so inadequate that we can, in using them, not even delimit clearly what we are talking about.

We may as well begin with the terms generally used to distinguish between the two opposed principles of the order of human collaboration, capitalism and socialism, both of which are misleading and politically biased. While intended to throw a certain light on these systems, they tell us nothing relevant about their character. The word 'capitalism' in particular (still unknown to Karl Marx in 1867 and never used by him) 'burst upon political debate as the natural opposite of socialism' only with Werner Sombart's explosive book *Der moderne Kapitalismus* in 1902 (Braudel, 1982a:227). Since this term suggests a system serving the special interests of the owners of capital, it naturally provoked the opposition of those who, as we have seen, were its main beneficiaries, the members of the proletariat. The proletariat was enabled by the activity of owners of capital to survive and increase, and was in a sense actually called into being by them. It is true that owners of capital made the extended order of human intercourse possible, and this might have led to some capitalists proudly accepting that name for the result of their efforts. It was nevertheless an unfortunate development in suggesting a clash of interests which does not really exist.

A somewhat more satisfactory name for the extended economic order of collaboration is the term 'market economy', imported from the German. Yet it too suffers from some serious disadvantages. In the first instance, the so-called market economy is not really an economy in the strict sense but a complex of large numbers of interacting individual economies with which it shares some but by no means all defining characteristics. If we give to the complex structures resulting from the interaction of individual economies a name that suggests that they are deliberate constructions, this yields the personification or animism to which, as we have seen, so many misconceptions of the processes of human interaction are due, and which we are at pains to escape. It is necessary to be constantly reminded that the economy the market produces is not really like products of deliberate human design but is a structure which, while in some respects resembling an economy, in other regards, particularly in not serving a unitary hierarchy of ends, differs fundamentally from a true economy.

A second disadvantage of the term market economy is that in English no convenient adjective can be derived from it, and such an expression indicating the appropriateness of particular actions is indeed needed in practice. Hence I proposed some time ago (1967/1978b:90) that we introduce a new technical term, one obtained from a Greek root that had already been used in a very similar connection. In 1838 Archbishop

Whately suggested 'catallactics' as a name for the theoretical science explaining the market order, and his suggestion has been revived from time to time, most recently by Ludwig von Mises. The adjective 'catallactic' is readily derived from Whately's coinage, and has already been used fairly widely. These terms are particularly attractive because the classical Greek word from which they stem, *katalattein* or *katalassein*, meant not only 'to exchange' but also 'to receive into the community' and 'to turn from enemy into friend', further evidence of the profound insight of the ancient Greeks in such matters (Liddell and Scott, 1940, s.v. *katallasso*). This led me to suggest that we form the term *catallaxy* to describe the object of the science we generally call economics, which then, following Whately, itself ought to be called catallactics. The usefulness of such an innovation has been confirmed by the former term's already having been adopted by some of my younger colleagues and I am convinced that its more general adoption might really contribute to the clarity of our discussion.

Our Animistic Vocabulary and the Confused Concept of 'Society'

As such examples illustrate all too well, in the study of human affairs difficulties of communication begin with the definition and naming of the very objects we wish to analyse. The chief terminological barrier to understanding, outranking in importance the other terms we have just discussed, is the expression 'society' itself – and not only inasmuch as it has, since Marx, been used to blur distinctions between governments and other 'institutions'. As a word used to describe a variety of systems of interconnections of human activities, 'society' falsely suggests that all such systems are of the same kind. It is also one of the oldest terms of this kind, as for example in the Latin *societas*, from *socius*, the personally known fellow or companion; and it has been used to describe both an actually existing state of affairs and a relation between individuals. As usually employed, it presupposes or implies a common pursuit of shared purposes that usually can be achieved only by conscious collaboration.

As we have seen, it is one of the necessary conditions of the extension of human cooperation beyond the limits of individual awareness that the range of such pursuits be increasingly governed not by shared purposes but by abstract rules of conduct whose observance brings it about that we more and more serve the needs of people whom we do not know and find our own needs similarly satisfied by unknown persons. Thus the more the range of human cooperation extends, the less does motivation within it correspond to the mental picture people have of what should happen in a 'society', and the more 'social' comes to be not the key word in a statement of the facts but the core of an appeal to an ancient, and now obsolete, ideal of general human behaviour. Any real appreciation of the difference between, on the one hand, what actually characterises individual behaviour in a particular group and, on the other, wishful thinking about what individual conduct *should* be (in accordance with older customs) is increasingly lost. Not only is any group of persons connected in practically any manner called a 'society', but it is concluded that any such group should behave as a primitive group of companions did.

Thus the word 'society' has become a convenient label denoting almost any group of people, a group about whose structure or reason for coherence nothing need be known – a makeshift phrase people resort to when they do not quite know what they are talking about. Apparently a people, a nation, a population, a company, an association, a group, a horde, a band, a tribe, the members of a race, of a religion, sport, entertainment, and the inhabitants of any particular place, all are, or constitute, societies.

To call by the same name such completely different formations as the companionship of individuals in constant personal contact and the structure formed by millions who are connected only by signals resulting from long and infinitely ramified chains of trade is not only factually misleading but also almost always contains a concealed desire to model this extended order on the intimate fellowship for which our emotions long. Bertrand de Jouvenel has well described this instinctive nostalgia for the small group – 'the milieu in which man is first found, which retains for him an infinite attraction: but any attempt to graft the same features on a large society is utopian and leads to tyranny' (1957:136).

The crucial difference overlooked in this confusion is that the small group can be led in its activities by agreed aims or the will of its members, while the extended order that is also a 'society' is formed into a concordant structure by its members' observance of similar rules of conduct in the pursuit of different individual purposes. The result of such diverse efforts under similar rules will indeed show a few characteristics resembling those of an individual organism possessing a brain or mind, or what such an organism deliberately arranges, but it is misleading to treat such a 'society' animistically, or to personify it by ascribing to it a will, an intention, or a design. Hence it is disturbing to find a serious contemporary scholar confessing that to any utilitarian 'society' must appear not 'as a plurality of persons . . . [but] as a sort of single great person' (Chapman, 1964:153).

113

The Weasel Word 'Social'

The noun 'society', misleading as it is, is relatively innocuous compared with the adjective 'social', which has probably become the most confusing expression in our entire moral and political vocabulary. This has happened only during the past hundred years, during which time its modern usages, and its power and influence, have expanded rapidly from Bismarckian Germany to cover the whole world. The confusion that it spreads, within the very area wherein it is most used, is partly due to its describing not only phenomena produced by various modes of cooperation among men, such as in a 'society', but also the kinds of actions that promote and serve such orders. From this latter usage it has increasingly been turned into an exhortation, a sort of guide-word for rationalist morals intended to displace traditional morals, and now increasingly supplants the word 'good' as a designation of what is morally right. As a result of this 'distinctly dichotomous' character, as *Webster's New Dictionary of Synonyms* appropriately puts it, factual and normative meanings of the word 'social' constantly alternate, and what at first seems a description imperceptibly turns into a prescription.

> On this particular matter, German usage influenced the American language more than English; for by the eighteen-eighties a group of German scholars known as the historical or ethical school of economic research had increasingly substituted the term 'social policy' for the term 'political economy' to designate the study of human interaction. One of the few not to be swept away by this new fashion, Leopold von Wiese, later remarked that only those who were young in the 'social age' – in the decades immediately before the Great War – can appreciate how strong at that time was the inclination to regard the 'social' sphere as a surrogate for religion. One of the most dramatic manifestations of this was the appearance of the so-called social pastors. But 'to be "social" ', Wiese insists, 'is not the same as being good or righteous or "righteous in the eyes of God" ' (1917). To some of Wiese's students we owe instructive historical studies on the spreading of the term 'social' (see my references in 1976:180).

The extraordinary variety of uses to which the word 'social' has since been put in English is brought home vividly when in the *Fontana Dictionary of Modern Thought* (1977), cited earlier in another context, is found, appropriately preceded by 'Soap Opera', a series of no less than thirty-five combinations of 'social' with some noun or other, from 'Social Action' to 'Social Wholes'. In a similar effort, R. Williams's *Key Words* (1976), the author, although generally referring the reader, with the conventional 'q.v.', to corresponding entries, departed from this practice with regard to 'social'. Apparently it would have been impractical for him to follow his policy here, and he simply had to abandon it. These examples led me for a while to note down all occurrences of 'social' that I encountered, thus producing the following instructive list of over one hundred and sixty nouns qualified by the adjective 'social':

accounting	action	adjustment
administration	affairs	agreement
age	animal	appeal
awareness	behaviour	being
body	causation	character
circle	climber	compact
composition	comprehension	concern
conception	conflict	conscience
consciousness	consideration	construction
contract	control	credit
cripples	critic (-que)	crusader
decision	demand	democracy
description	development	dimension
discrimation	disease	disposition
distance	duty	economy
end	entity	environment
epistemology	ethics	etiquette
event	evil	fact
factors	fascism	force
framework	function	gathering
geography	goal	good
graces	group	harmony
health	history	ideal
implication	inadequacy	independence
inferiority	institution	insurance
intercourse	justice	knowledge
laws	leader	life
market economy	medicine	migration
mind	morality	morals
needs	obligation	opportunity
order	organism	orientation
outcast	ownership	partner
passion	peace	pension
person	philosophy	pleasure
point of view	policy	position
power	priority	privilege

problem	process	product
progress	property	psychology
rank	realism	realm
Rechtsstaat	recognition	reform
relations	remedy	research
response	responsibility	revolution
right	role	rule of law
satisfaction	science	security
service	signals	significance
Soziolekt (group speech)	solidarity	spirit
structure	stability	standing
status	struggle	student
studies	survey	system
talent	teleology	tenets
tension	theory	thinkers
thought	traits	usefulness
utility	value	views
virtue	want	waste
wealth	will	work
worker	world	

Many of the combinations given here are even more widely used in a negative, critical form: thus 'social adjustment' becomes 'social maladjustment', and the same for 'social disorder', 'social injustice', 'social insecurity', 'social instability', and so on.

It is difficult to conclude from this list alone whether the word 'social' has acquired so many different meanings as to become useless as a tool of communication. However this may be, its practical effect is quite clear and at least threefold. First, it tends pervertedly to insinuate a notion that we have seen from previous chapters to be misconceived – namely, that what has been brought about by the impersonal and spontaneous processes of the extended order is actually the result of deliberate human creation. Second, following from this, it appeals to men to redesign what they never could have designed at all. And third, it also has acquired the power to empty the nouns it qualifies of their meaning.

In this last effect, it has in fact become the most harmful instance of what, after Shakespeare's 'I can suck melancholy out of a song, as a weasel suck eggs' (*As You Like It*, II,5), some Americans call a 'weasel word'. As a weasel is alleged to be able to empty an egg without leaving a visible sign, so can these words deprive of content any term to which they are prefixed while seemingly leaving them untouched. A weasel word is used to draw the teeth from a concept one is obliged to employ, but from which one wishes to eliminate all implications that challenge one's ideological premises.

On current American usage of the expression see the late Mario Pei's *Weasel Words: The Art of Saying What You Don't Mean* (1978), which credits Theodore Roosevelt with having coined the term in 1918, thus suggesting that seventy years ago American statesmen were remarkably well educated. Yet the reader will not find in that book the prize weasel word 'social'.

Though abuse of the word 'social' is international, it has taken perhaps its most extreme forms in West Germany where the constitution of 1949 employed the expression *sozialer Rechtsstaat* (social rule of law) and whence the conception of 'social market economy' has spread – in a sense which its populariser Ludwig Erhard certainly never intended. (He once assured me in conversation that to him the market economy did not have to be *made* social but was so already as a result of its origin.) But while the rule of law and the market are, at the start, fairly clear concepts, the attribute 'social' empties them of any clear meaning. From these uses of the word 'social', German scholars have come to the conclusion that their government is constitutionally subject to the *Sozialstaatsprinzip*, which means little less than that the rule of law has been suspended. Likewise, such German scholars see a conflict between *Rechtsstaat* and *Sozialstaat* and entrench the *soziale Rechtsstaat* in their constitution – one, I may perhaps say, that was written by Fabian muddle-heads inspired by the nineteenth-century inventor of 'National Socialism', Friedrich Naumann (H. Maier, 1972:8).

Similarly, the term 'democracy' used to have a fairly clear meaning; yet 'social democracy' not only served as the name for the radical Austro-Marxism of the inter-war period but now has been chosen in Britain as a label for a political party committed to a sort of Fabian socialism. Yet the traditional term for what is now called the 'social state' was 'benevolent despotism', and the very real problem of achieving such despotism democratically, i.e., while preserving individual freedom, is simply wished away by the concoction 'social democracy'.

'Social Justice' and 'Social Rights'

Much the worst use of 'social', one that wholly destroys the meaning of any word it qualifies, is in the almost universally used phrase 'social justice'. Though I have dealt with this particular matter already at some length, particularly in the second volume on *The Mirage of Social Justice* in my *Law, Legislation and Liberty*, I must at least briefly state the point again here, since it plays such an important part in arguments for and against socialism. The phrase 'social justice' is, as a distinguished

117

man more courageous than I bluntly expressed it long ago, simply 'a semantic fraud from the same stable as People's Democracy' (Curran, 1958:8). The alarming extent to which the term seems already to have perverted the thinking of the younger generation is shown by a recent Oxford doctor's thesis on *Social Justice* (Miller, 1976), in which the traditional conception of justice is referred to by the extraordinary remark that 'there appears to be a category of private justice'.

I have seen it suggested that 'social' applies to everything that reduces or removes differences of income. But why call such action 'social'? Perhaps because it is a method of securing majorities, that is, votes in addition to those one expects to get for other reasons? This does seem to be so, but it also means of course that every exhortation to us to be 'social' is an appeal for a further step towards the 'social justice' of socialism. Thus use of the term 'social' becomes virtually equivalent to the call for 'distributive justice'. This is, however, irreconcilable with a competitive market order, and with growth or even maintenance of population and of wealth. Thus people have come, through such errors, to call 'social' what is the main obstacle to the very maintenance of 'society'. 'Social' should really be called 'anti-social'.

It is probably true that men would be happier about their economic conditions if they felt that the relative positions of individuals were just. Yet the whole idea behind distributive justice – that each individual ought to receive what he morally deserves – is meaningless in the extended order of human cooperation (or the catallaxy), because the available product (its size, and even its existence) depends on what is in one sense a morally indifferent way of allocating its parts. For reasons already explored, moral desert cannot be determined objectively, and in any case the adaptation of the larger whole to facts yet to be discovered requires that we accept that 'success is based on results, not on motivation' (Alchian, 1950:213). Any extended system of cooperation must adapt itself constantly to changes in its natural environment (which include the life, health and strength of its members); the demand that only changes with just effect should occur is ridiculous. It is nearly as ridiculous as the belief that deliberate organisation of response to such changes can be just. Mankind could neither have reached nor could now maintain its present numbers without an inequality that is neither determined by, nor reconcilable with, any deliberate moral judgements. Effort of course will improve individual chances, but it alone cannot secure results. The envy of those who have tried just as hard, although fully understandable, works against the common interest. Thus, if the common interest is *really* our interest, we must not give in to this very human instinctual trait, but instead allow the market process to determine the reward. Nobody can ascertain, save through the market, the size of an individual's contribution to the overall product, nor can it otherwise be determined how much remuneration must be tendered to someone to enable him to choose the activity which will add most to the flow of goods and services offered at large. Of course if the latter should be considered morally good, then the market turns out to produce a supremely moral result.

Mankind is split into two hostile groups by promises that have no realisable content. The sources of this conflict cannot be dissipated by compromise, for every concession to factual error merely creates more unrealisable expectations. Yet, an anti-capitalist ethic continues to develop on the basis of errors by people who condemn the wealth-generating institutions to which they themselves owe their existence. Pretending to be lovers of freedom, they condemn several property, contract, competition, advertising, profit, and even money itself. Imagining that their reason can tell them how to arrange human efforts to serve their innate wishes better, they themselves pose a grave threat to civilisation.

EIGHT

THE EXTENDED ORDER AND POPULATION GROWTH

The most decisive of the prosperity of any country is the increase of the number of its inhabitants.

Adam Smith

The Malthusian Scare: The Fear of Overpopulation

I have been attempting to explain how the extended order of human cooperation has evolved despite opposition from our instincts, despite fear of all the uncertainties inherent in spontaneous processes, despite widespread economic ignorance, and despite the distillation of all these in movements that seek to use allegedly rational means to achieve genuinely atavistic ends. I have also maintained that the extended order would collapse, and that much of our population would suffer and die, if such movements ever did truly succeed in displacing the market. Like it or not, the current world population already exists. Destroying its material foundation in order to attain the 'ethical' or instinctually gratifying improvements advocated by socialists would be tantamount to condoning the death of billions and the impoverishment of the rest. (See also my 1954/1967:208; and 1983:25–29.)

The close connection between population size and the presence of, and benefits of, certain evolved practices, institutions, and forms of human interaction is hardly a new discovery. That 'as it is the power of exchanging that gives occasion to the division of labour, so the extent of this division must always be limited by the extent of this power, or, in other words, by the extent of the market' was one of Adam Smith's profoundest insights (1776/1976:31); cf. also the two 'Fragments on the Division of Labour' in *Lectures on Jurisprudence* (1978:582–586). That those following competitive market practices would, as they grew in numbers, displace others who followed different customs, was also seen early. Following John Locke's similar claim in the *Second Treatise* (1690/1887), the American historian James Sullivan remarked, as early as 1795, how the native Americans had been displaced by European colonists, and that now five hundred thinking beings could prosper in the same area where previously only a single savage could 'drag out a hungry existence' as a hunter (1795:139). (The native American tribes that continued to engage primarily in hunting were displaced also from another direction: by tribes that had learnt to practise agriculture.)

Although the displacement of one group by another, and of one set of practices by another, has often been bloody, it does not need always to be so. No doubt the course of events differed from place to place, and we can hardly go into the details here, but one can imagine many different sequences of events. In some places invaded, as it were, by the extended order, those following new practices, who could extract more from the given land, would often be able to offer other occupants, in return for access to their land (without the occupants having to do any work at all, and without the 'invaders' having to use force), nearly as much as, and sometimes even more than, these occupants had obtained by hard toil. On the other hand, the very density of their own settlements would have enabled more advanced people to resist attempts to evict them from extensive territories that they had used, and needed, during periods when they themselves had practised more primitive methods of land use. Many of these processes may then have happened entirely peacefully, although the greater military strength of commercially organised people will often have accelerated the process.

Even if the extension of the market and the growth of population could be achieved entirely by peaceful means, well-informed and thoughtful people are, nevertheless, increasingly reluctant today to continue to accept the association between population growth and the rise of civilisation. Quite the contrary, as they contemplate our present population density and, more especially, the acceleration in the rate of population increase during the past three hundred years, they have become highly alarmed, and construe the prospect of increasing growth of population as a disaster of nightmare quality. Even a sensible philosopher like A. G. N. Flew (1967:60) praised Julian Huxley for recognising early, 'before this was even as widely admitted as it now is, that human fertility represents the number one threat to the present and future welfare of the human race'.

I have been contending that socialism constitutes a threat to the present and future welfare of the human race, in the sense that neither socialism nor any other known substitute for the market order could sustain the current population of the world. But reactions like the one just quoted, as often as not made by people who do not themselves advocate socialism, suggest that a market order that produces, and is produced by, such a large population *also* poses a serious threat to the welfare of mankind. Obviously this conflict must now be addressed.

The modern idea that population growth threatens worldwide pauperisation is simply a mistake. It is largely a consequence of oversimplifying the Malthusian theory of population; Thomas Malthus's theory made a reasonable first approach to the problem in his own time, but modern conditions make it irrelevant. Malthus's assumption that human labour could be regarded as a more or less homogeneous factor of production (i.e., wage labour was all of the same kind, employed in agriculture, with the same tools and the same opportunities) was not far from the truth in the economic order that then existed (a theoretical two-factor economy). For Malthus, who was also one of the first discoverers of the law of decreasing returns, this must have indicated that every increase in the number of labourers would lead to a reduction of what is now called marginal productivity, and therefore of worker income, particularly once the best land had been occupied by plots of optimum size. (On the relation between Malthus's two theorems see McCleary, 1953:111.)

This ceases to be true, however, under the changed conditions we have been discussing, wherein labour is not homogeneous but is diversified and specialised. With the intensification of exchange, and improving techniques of communication and transportation, an increase of numbers and density of occupation makes division of labour advantageous, leads to radical diversification, differentiation and specialisation, makes it possible to develop new factors of production, and heightens productivity (see chapters two and three above, and also below). Different skills, natural or acquired, become distinct scarce factors, often manifoldly complementary; this makes it worthwhile to workers to acquire new skills which will then fetch different market prices. Voluntary specialisation is guided by differences in expected rewards. Thus labour may yield increasing rather than decreasing returns. A denser population can also employ techniques and technology that would have been useless in more thinly occupied regions; and if such technologies have already been developed elsewhere they may well be imported and adopted rapidly (provided the required capital can be obtained). Even the bare fact of living peacefully in constant contact with larger numbers makes it possible to utilise available resources more fully.

When, in such a way, labour ceases to be a homogeneous factor of production, Malthus's conclusions cease to apply. Rather, an increase of population may now, because of further differentiation, make *still further* increases of population possible, and *for indefinite periods* population increase may be both self-accelerating and a pre-requisite for any advance in both material and (because of the individuation made possible) spiritual civilisation.

It is, then, not simply more men, but more different men, which brings an increase in productivity. Men have become powerful because they have become so different: new possibilities of specialisation – depending not so much on any increase in individual intelligence but on growing differentiation of individuals – provide the basis for a more successful use of the earth's resources. This in turn requires an extension of the network of indirect reciprocal services which the signalling mechanism of the market secures. As the market reveals ever new opportunities of specialisation, the two-factor model, with its Malthusian conclusions, becomes increasingly inapplicable.

The widely prevailing fear that the growth of population that attends and fosters all this is apt to lead to general impoverishment and disaster is thus largely due to the misunderstanding of a statistical calculation.

This is not to deny that an increase of population may lead to a reduction of average incomes. But this possibility is also misinterpreted – the misinterpretation here being due to conflating the average income of a number of existing people in different income classes with the average income of a later, larger number of people. The proletariat are an *additional* population that, without new opportunities of employment, would never have grown up. The fall in average income occurs simply because great population growth generally involves a greater increase of the poorer, rather than the richer, strata of a population. But it is incorrect to conclude that anybody needs to have *become* poorer in the process. No single member of an existing community need to have become poorer (though some well-to-do people are likely, in the process, to be displaced by some of the newcomers and to descend to a lower level). Indeed, everyone who was *already* there might have grown somewhat richer; and yet average incomes may have decreased if large numbers of poor people have been *added* to those formerly present. It is trivially true that a reduction of the average is compatible with all income groups having increased in numbers, but with higher ones increasing in numbers less than the lower ones. That is, if the base of the income pyramid grows more than its height, the average income of the increased total will be smaller.

But it would be more accurate to conclude from this that the process of growth benefits the larger number of the poor more than the smaller number of the rich. Capitalism created the possibility of employment. It created the conditions wherein people who have not been endowed by their parents with the tools and land needed to maintain themselves and their offspring could be so equipped by others, to their mutual benefit. For the process enabled people to live poorly, and to have children, who otherwise, without the opportunity for productive work, could hardly even have grown to maturity and multiplied: it brought into being and kept millions alive who otherwise would not have lived at all and who, if they had lived for a time, could not have afforded to procreate. In this

123

way the poor benefited more from the process. Karl Marx was thus right to claim that *'capitalism' created the proletariat: it gave and gives them life.*

Thus the whole idea that the rich wrested away from the poor what, without such acts of violence would, or at least might, belong to them, is absurd.

The size of the stock of capital of a people, together with its accumulated traditions and practices for extracting and communicating information, determine whether that people can maintain large numbers. People will be employed, and materials and tools produced to serve future needs of unknown persons, only if those who can invest capital to bridge the interval between present outlay and future return will gain an increment from doing this which is at least as great as what they could have obtained from other uses of that capital.

Thus without the rich – without those who accumulated capital – those poor who could exist at all would be very much poorer indeed, scratching a livelihood from marginal lands on which every drought would kill most of the children they would be trying to raise. The creation of capital altered such conditions more than anything else. As the capitalist became able to employ other people for his own purposes, his ability to feed them served both him and them. This ability increased further as some individuals were able to employ others not just directly to satisfy their own needs but to trade goods and services with countless others. Thus property, contract, trade, and the use of capital did not simply benefit a minority.

Envy and ignorance lead people to regard possessing more than one needs for current consumption as a matter for censure rather than merit. Yet the idea that such capital must be accumulated 'at the expense of others' is a throwback to economic views that, however obvious they may seem to some, are actually groundless, and make an accurate understanding of economic development impossible.

The Regional Character of the Problem

Another source of misunderstanding is the tendency to think of population growth in purely global terms. The population problem must be seen as regional, with different aspects in different areas. The real problem is whether the numbers of inhabitants of particular regions tend, for whatever reason, to outgrow the resources of their own areas (including the resources they can use to trade).

As long as an increase in population has been made possible by the growing productivity of the populations in the regions concerned, or by more effective utilisation of their resources, and not by deliberate artificial support of this growth from outside, there is little cause for concern. Morally, we have as little right to prevent the growth of population in other parts of the world as we have a duty to assist it. On the other hand, a moral conflict may indeed arise if materially advanced countries continue to assist and indeed even subsidise the growth of populations in regions, such as perhaps the Sahel zone in Central Africa, where there appears to exist little prospect that its present population, let alone an increased one, will in the foreseeable future be able to maintain itself by its own efforts. With any attempt to maintain populations beyond the volume at which accumulated capital could still be currently reproduced, the number that could be maintained would diminish. Unless we interfere, only such populations will increase further as can feed themselves. The advanced countries, by assisting populations such as that in the Sahel to increase, are arousing expectations, creating conditions involving obligations, and thus assuming a grave responsibility on which they are very likely sooner or later to default. Man is not omnipotent; and recognising the limits of his powers may enable him to approach closer to realising his wishes than following natural impulses to remedy remote suffering about which he can, unfortunately, do little if anything.

In any case, there is no danger whatever that, in any foreseeable future with which we can be concerned, the population of the world as a whole will outgrow its raw material resources, and every reason to assume that inherent forces will stop such a process long before that could happen. (See the studies of Julian L. Simon (1977, 1981a & b), Esther Boserup (1981), Douglas North (1973, 1981) and Peter Bauer (1981), as well as my own 1954:15 and 1967:208.)

For there are, in the temperate zones of all continents except Europe, wide regions which can not merely bear an increase in population, but whose inhabitants can hope to approach the standards of general wealth, comfort, and civilisation that the 'Western' world has already reached only by increasing the density of their occupation of their land and the intensity of exploitation of its resources. In these regions the population must multiply if its members are to achieve the standards for which they strive. It is in their own interest to increase their numbers, and it would be presumptuous, and hardly defensible morally, to advise them, let alone to coerce them, to hold down their numbers. While serious problems may arise if we attempt indiscriminately to preserve all human lives everywhere, others cannot legitimately object to an increase in numbers on the part of a group that is able to maintain its own numbers by its own efforts. Inhabitants of countries already wealthy hardly have any right to call for an 'end to growth' (as did the Club of Rome or the later production *Global 2000*), or to obstruct the countries in question, which rightly resent any such policies.

Some notions that attend such recommended policies for restricting population – for example, that advanced peoples should turn parts of the territories inhabited by still undeveloped people into a sort of nature park – are indeed outrageous. The idyllic image of happy primitives who enjoy their rural poverty and will gladly forego the development that alone can give many of them access to what they have come to regard as the benefits of civilisation is based on fantasy. Such benefits do, as we have seen, demand certain instinctual and other sacrifices. But less advanced people must decide for themselves, individually, whether material comfort and advanced culture is worth the sacrifices involved. They should, of course, not be forced to modernise; nor should they be prevented, through a policy of isolation, from seeking the opportunities of modernisation.

With the sole exception of instances where the increase of the numbers of the poor has led governments to redistribute incomes in their favour, there is no instance in history wherein an increase of population reduced the standards of life of those in that population who had already achieved various levels. As Simon has convincingly argued, 'There are not now, and there never have been, any empirical data showing that population growth or size or density have a negative effect on the standard of living' (1981a:18, and see also his major works on this subject, 1977 and 1981b).

Diversity and Differentiation

Differentiation is the key to understanding population growth, and we should pause to expand on this crucial point. The unique achievement of man, leading to many of his other distinct characteristics, is his differentiation and diversity. Apart from a few other species in which selection artificially imposed by man has produced comparable diversity, man's diversification is unparalleled. This occurred because, in the course of natural selection, humans developed a highly efficient organ for learning from their fellows. This has made the increase of man's numbers, over much of his history, not, as in other instances, self-limiting, but rather self-stimulating. Human population grew in a sort of chain reaction in which greater density of occupation of territory tended to produce new opportunities for specialisation and thus led to an increase of individual productivity and in turn to a further increase of numbers. There also developed among such large numbers of people not only a variety of innate attributes but also an enormous variety of streams of cultural traditions among which their great intelligence enabled them to select – particularly during their prolonged adolescence. The greater

126

part of humankind can now maintain itself just because its members are so flexible, just because there are so many different individuals whose different gifts enable them to differentiate themselves from one another even further by absorbing a boundless variety of combinations of differing streams of traditions.

The diversity for which increasing density provided new opportunities was essentially that of labour and skills, of information and knowledge, of property and incomes. The process is neither simple nor causal nor predictable, for at each step increasing population density merely creates unrealised possibilities which may or may not be discovered and realised rapidly. Only where some earlier population had already passed through this stage and its example could be imitated, could the process be very rapid. Learning proceeds through a multiplicity of channels and presupposes a great variety of individual positions and connections among groups and individuals through which possibilities of collaboration emerge.

Once people learn to take advantage of new opportunities offered by increased density of population (not only because of the specialisation brought about by division of labour, knowledge and property, but also by some individual accumulation of new forms of capital), this becomes the basis of yet further increases. Thanks to multiplication, differentiation, communication and interaction over increasing distances, and transmission through time, mankind has become a distinct entity preserving certain structural features that can produce effects beneficial to a further increase of numbers.

So far as we know, the extended order is probably the most complex structure in the universe – a structure in which biological organisms that are already highly complex have acquired the capacity to learn, to assimilate, parts of suprapersonal traditions enabling them to adapt themselves from moment to moment into an ever-changing structure possessing an order of a still higher level of complexity. Step by step, momentary impediments to further population increase are penetrated, increases in population provide a foundation for further ones, and so on, leading to a progressive and cumulative process that does not end before all the fertile or richly endowed parts of the earth are similarly densely occupied.

The Centre and the Periphery

And it may indeed end there: I do not think that the much-dreaded population explosion – leading to 'standing room only' – is going to occur. The whole story of population growth may now be approaching its end, or at least approaching a very new level. For the highest population growth has never taken place in developed market economies but always on the peripheries of developed economies, among those poor who had no fertile land and equipment that would have enabled them to maintain themselves, but to whom 'capitalists' offered new opportunities for survival.

These peripheries are, however, disappearing. Moreover, there are hardly any countries left to enter the periphery: the explosive process of population expansion has, during the last generation or so, very nearly reached the last corners of the earth.

Consequently there is strong reason to doubt the accuracy of extrapolating the trend of the last several centuries – of an indefinitely increasing acceleration of population growth – into the indefinite future. We may hope and expect that once the remaining reservoir of people who are now entering the extended order is exhausted, the growth of their numbers, which distresses people so much, will gradually recede. After all, no fairly wealthy group shows any such tendency. We do not know enough to say when the turning point will be reached, but we can fairly assume that it will be very long indeed before we approach the horrors which the fancy of the ineluctable indefinite increase of mankind conjures up.

I suspect that the problem is already diminishing: that the population growth rate is now approaching, or has already reached, its maximum, and will not increase much further but will decline. One cannot of course say for certain, but it appears that – even if this has not already occurred – some time in the last decade of this century population growth will reach a maximum and that, afterwards, it will decline unless there is deliberate intervention to stimulate it.

Already in the mid 1960's, the annual rate of growth of the developing regions peaked at around 2.4 percent, and began to decline to the present level of around 2.1 percent. And the population growth rate in more developed regions was already on the decline by this same time. In the mid 'sixties, then, population seems to have reached, and then retreated from, an all-time high annual growth rate (United Nations, 1980, and J. E. Cohen, 1984:50-51). As Cohen writes: 'humankind has begun to practice or to experience the restraint that governs all its fellow species.'

The processes at work may become more comprehensible if we take a closer look at the populations at the peripheries of the developing economies. The best examples are perhaps to be found in those fast-growing cities of the developing world – Mexico City, Cairo, Calcutta, Sao Paulo or Jakarta, Caracas, Lagos, Bombay – where the population has doubled or more over a short span and where old city centers tend to be surrounded by shanty towns or 'bidonvilles'.

The increase of population taking place in these cities stems from the fact that people living on peripheries of market economies, while already profiting from their participation in them (through, for example, access to more advanced medicine, to better information of all sorts, and to advanced economic institutions and practices), have nonetheless not adapted fully to the traditions, morality, and customs of these economies. For example, they still may practice customs of procreation stemming from circumstances outside the market economy where, for instance, the first response of poor people to a slight increase of wealth had been to produce a number of descendants at least sufficient to provide for them in their old age. These old customs are now gradually, and in some places even quickly, disappearing, and these peripheral groups, particularly those closest to the core, are absorbing traditions that allow them better to regulate their propagation. After all, the growing commercial centers become magnets in part just because they provide models of how to achieve through imitation what many people desire.

These shanty towns, which are interesting in themselves, also illustrate several other themes developed earlier. For example, the population of the countryside around these cities has not been depleted at the expense of the shanty towns; usually it too has profited from the growth of the cities. The cities offered sustenance to millions who otherwise would have died or never been born had they (or their parents) not migrated to them. Those who did migrate to the cities (or to their peripheries) were led there neither by the benevolence of the city folk in offering jobs and equipment nor by the benevolent advice of their better-off country 'neighbours', but rather by following rumours about other unknown poor folk (perhaps in some remote mountain valley) who were saved by being drawn into the growing towns by news of paid work available there. Ambition, even greed, for a better life, not beneficence, preserved these lives: yet it did better than beneficence could have done. The people from the countryside learned from market signals – although they could hardly have understood the matter in such abstract terms – that income not currently consumed by rich men in the cities was being used to provide others with tools or livelihood in payment for work, enabling people to survive who had not inherited arable land and the tools to cultivate it.

Of course it may be hard for some to accept that those living in these shanty towns deliberately chose them over the countryside (about which people have such romantic feelings) as places of sustenance. Yet, as with the Irish and English peasants Engels found in the Manchester slums of his own time, that is what happened.

The squalor of these peripheral areas is primarily due to the very

129

economic marginality that dictated residence there rather than in the countryside. Also not to be ignored are the adverse 'cyclical' effects of third-world governments' attempts to manage their economies, and of the ability of these governments to remove employment opportunities from peripheral groups as concessions to established labour interests or misguided social reformers.

Finally – and here one may sometimes witness the selection process at something like first hand, and in its most naked form – the effects of commercial morals do not fall most harshly and visibly on those who have already learnt to practise them in a relatively more advanced form, but rather on newcomers who have not yet learnt how to cope with them. Those who live on the peripheries do not yet fully observe the new practices (and thus are almost always perceived as 'undesirable' and often thought even to border on the criminal). They are also experiencing personally the first impact that some practices of more advanced civilisation exert on people who still feel and think according to the morality of the tribe and village. However painful for them this process may be, they too, or they especially, benefit from the division of labour formed by the practices of the business classes; and many of them gradually change their ways, only then improving the quality of their lives. At least a minimal change of conduct on their part will be a condition for their being permitted to enter the larger established group and gradually to gain an increasing share in its total product.

For the numbers kept alive by differing systems of rules decide which system will dominate. These systems of rules will not necessarily be those that the masses (of which the shanty-town dwellers are only a dramatic example) themselves have already fully adopted, but those followed by a nucleus around whose periphery increasing numbers gather to participate in gains from the growing total product. Those who do at least partially adopt, and benefit from, the practices of the extended order often do so without being aware of the sacrifices such changes will also eventually involve. Nor is it only primitive country folk who have had to learn hard lessons: military conquerors who lorded over a subject population and even destroyed its elite often later had to learn, sometimes to their regret, that to enjoy local benefits required adopting local practices.

Capitalism Gave Life to the Proletariat

We may in our remaining sections perhaps draw together some of our main arguments and note some of their implications.

If we ask what men most owe to the moral practices of those who are called capitalists the answer is: their very lives. Socialist accounts which ascribe the existence of the proletariat to an exploitation of groups

130

formerly able to maintain themselves are entirely fictional. Most individuals who now make up the proletariat could not have existed before others provided them with means to subsist. Although these folk may *feel* exploited, and politicians may arouse and play on these feelings to gain power, most of the Western proletariat, and most of the millions of the developing world, owe their existence to opportunities that advanced countries have created for them. All this is not confined to Western countries or the developing world. Communist countries such as Russia would be starving today if their populations were not kept alive by the Western world – although the leaders of these countries would be hard put to admit publicly that we can support the current population of the world, including that of the communist countries, only if we maintain successfully and improve the basis of private property which makes our extended order possible.

Capitalism also introduced a new form of obtaining income from production that *liberates* people in making them, and often their progeny as well, independent of family groups or tribes. This is so even if capitalism is sometimes prevented from providing all it might for those who wish to take advantage of it by monopolies of organised groups of workers, 'unions', which create an artificial scarcity of their kind of work by preventing those willing to do such work for a lower wage from doing so.

The general advantage of replacing concrete particular purposes by abstract rules manifests itself clearly in cases like these. Nobody anticipated what was going to happen. Neither a conscious desire to make the human species grow as fast as possible nor concern for particular known lives produced that result. It was not always even those who first initiated new practices (saving, private property, and such like) whose physical offspring thus gained better chances of surviving. For these practices do not preserve *particular* lives but rather increase the *chances* (or prospects or probabilities) of more rapid propagation of the *group*. Such results were no more desired than foreseen. Some of these practices may indeed have involved a decrease in esteem for some individual lives, a preparedness to sacrifice by infanticide, to abandon the old and sick, or to kill the dangerous, in order to improve the prospects of maintaining and multiplying the rest.

We can hardly claim that to increase mankind is good in some absolute sense. We submit only that this effect, increase of particular populations following particular rules, led to the selection of those practices whose dominance has become the cause of further multiplication. (Nor, as we saw in chapter one, is it suggested that developed morals that restrain and suppress certain innate feelings should wholly displace these feelings. Our inborn instincts are still important in our relations to our immediate neighbours, and in certain other situations as well.)

Yet if the market economy did indeed prevail over other types of order because it enabled those groups that adopted its basic rules the better to multiply, then *the calculation in market values is a calculation in terms of lives*: individuals guided by this calculation did what most helped to increase their numbers, although this could hardly have been their intention.

The Calculus of Costs Is a Calculus of Lives

Though the concept of a 'calculus of lives' cannot be taken literally, it is more than a metaphor. There may be no simple quantitative relationships governing the preservation of human lives by economic action, but the importance of the ultimate effects of market conduct can hardly be overrated. Yet several qualifications have to be added. For the most part, only *unknown* lives will count as so many units when it is a question of sacrificing a few lives in order to serve a larger number elsewhere.

Even if we do not like to face the fact, we constantly have to make such decisions. Unknown individual lives, in public or private decisions, are not absolute values, and the builder of motor roads or of hospitals or electric equipment will never carry precautions against lethal accidents to the maximum, because by avoiding costs this would cause elsewhere, overall risks to human lives can be much reduced. When the army surgeon after a battle engages in 'triage' – when he lets one die who might be saved, because in the time he would have to devote to saving him he could save three other lives (see Hardin, 1980:59, who defines 'triage' as 'the procedure which saves the maximum of lives') – he is acting on a calculus of lives. This is another instance of how the alternative between saving more or fewer lives shapes our views, even if only as vague feelings about what ought to be done. The requirement of preserving the maximum number of lives is not that all individual lives be regarded as equally important. It may be more important to save the life of the doctor, in our example above, than to save the lives of any particular one of his patients: otherwise none might survive. Some lives are evidently more important in that they create or preserve other lives. The good hunter or defender of the community, the fertile mother and perhaps even the wise old man may be more important than most babies and most of the aged. On the preservation of the life of a good chief large numbers of other lives may depend. And the highly productive may be more valuable to the community than other adult individuals. *It is not the present number of lives that evolution will tend to maximise but the prospective stream of future lives.* If in a group all men of fertile age, or all such women, and the required numbers to defend and feed them, were preserved, the prospects of future growth would hardly

132

be affected, whereas the death of all females under forty-five would destroy all possibility of preserving the strain.

But if for this reason all unknown lives must count equally in the extended order – and in our own ideals we have closely approached this aim so far as government action is concerned – this aim has never governed behaviour in the small group or in our innate responses. Thus one is led to raise the question of the morality or goodness of the principle.

Yet, as with every other organism, the main 'purpose' to which man's physical make-up as well as his traditions are adapted is to produce other human beings. In this he has succeeded amazingly, and his conscious striving will have its most lasting effect only so far as, with or without his knowledge, it contributes to this result. There is no real point in asking whether those of his actions which do so contribute are really 'good', particularly if thus it is intended to inquire whether we *like* the results. For, as we have seen, we have never been able to choose our morals. Though there is a tendency to interpret goodness in a utilitarian way, to claim that 'good' is what brings about desired results, this claim is neither true nor useful. Even if we restrict ourselves to common usage, we find that the word 'good' generally refers to what tradition tells us we ought to do without knowing why – which is not to deny that justifications are always being invented for particular traditions. We can however perfectly well ask which among the many and conflicting rules that tradition treats as good tend, under particular conditions, to preserve and multiply those groups that follow them.

Life Has No Purpose But Itself

Life exists only so long as it provides for its own continuance. Whatever men live *for*, today most live only *because* of the market order. We have become civilised by the increase of our numbers just as civilisation made that increase possible: we can be few and savage, or many and civilised. If reduced to its population of ten thousand years ago, mankind could not preserve civilisation. Indeed, even if knowledge already gained were preserved in libraries, men could make little use of it without numbers sufficient to fill the jobs demanded for extensive specialisation and division of labour. All knowledge available in books would not save ten thousand people spared somewhere after an atomic holocaust from having to return to a life of hunters and gatherers, although it would probably shorten the total amount of time that humankind would have to remain in such a condition.

When people began to build better than they knew because they began to subordinate concrete common goals to abstract rules that enabled them to participate in a process of orderly collaboration that nobody could survey or arrange, and which no one could have predicted, they created situations unintended and often undesired. We may not like the fact that our rules were shaped mainly by their suitability for increasing our numbers, but we have little choice in the matter now (if we ever did), for we must deal with a situation that has already been brought into being. So many people already exist; and only a market economy can keep the bulk of them alive. Because of the rapid transfer of information, men everywhere now know what high standards of living are possible. Most of those who live in some more thinly settled places can hope to reach such standards only by multiplying and settling their regions more densely – so increasing even further the numbers that can be kept alive by a market economy.

Since we can preserve and secure even our present numbers only by adhering to the same general kinds of principles, it is our duty – unless we truly wish to condemn millions to starvation – to resist the claims of creeds that tend to destroy the basic principles of these morals, such as the institution of several property.

In any case, our desires and wishes are largely irrelevant. Whether we *desire* further increases of production and population or not, we must – merely to maintain existing numbers and wealth, and to protect them as best we can against calamity – strive after what, under favourable conditions, will continue to lead, at least for some time, and in many places, to further increases.

While I have not intended to evaluate the issue whether, if we had the choice, we would want to choose civilisation, examining issues of population raises two relevant points. First, the spectre of a population explosion that would make most lives miserable appears, as we have seen, to be unfounded. Once this danger is removed, if one considers the realities of 'bourgeois' life – but not utopian demands for a life free of all conflict, pain, lack of fulfilment, and, indeed, morality – one might think the pleasures and stimulations of civilisation not a bad bargain for those who do not yet enjoy them. But the question of whether we are better off civilised than not is probably unanswerable in any final way through such speculation. The second point is that the only thing close to an objective assessment of the issue is to see what people do when they are given the choice – as we are not. The readiness with which ordinary people of the Third World – as opposed to Western-educated intellectuals – appear to embrace the opportunities offered them by the extended order, even if it means inhabiting for a time shanty towns at the periphery, complements evidence regarding the reactions of European peasants to the introduction of urban capitalism, indicating that people will usually choose civilisation if they have the choice.

NINE

RELIGION AND THE GUARDIANS
OF TRADITION

Religion, even in its crudest form, gave a sanction to the rules of morality long before the age of artificial reasoning and philosophy.

Adam Smith

And others called it want of sense
Always to rail at what they loved.

Bernard Mandeville

Natural Selection from Among the Guardians of Tradition

In closing this work, I would like to make a few informal remarks – they are intended as no more than that – about the connection between the argument of this book and the role of religious belief. These remarks may be unpalatable to some intellectuals because they suggest that, in their own long-standing conflict with religion, they were partly mistaken – and very much lacking in appreciation.

This book has shown mankind as torn between two states of being. On one hand are the kinds of attitudes and emotions appropriate to behaviour in the small groups wherein mankind lived for more than a hundred thousand years, wherein known fellows learnt to serve one another, and to pursue common aims. Curiously, these archaic, more primitive attitudes and emotions are now supported by much of rationalism, and by the empiricism, hedonism, and socialism associated with it. On the other hand there is the more recent development in cultural evolution wherein we no longer chiefly serve known fellows or pursue common ends, but where institutions, moral systems, and traditions have evolved that have produced and now keep alive many times more people than existed before the dawn of civilisation, people who are engaged, largely peacefully though competitively, in pursuing thousands of different ends of their own choosing in collaboration with thousands of persons whom they will never know.

How can such a thing have happened? How could traditions which people do not like or understand, whose effects they usually do not appreciate and can neither see nor foresee, and which they are still

135

ardently combating, continue to have been passed on from generation to generation?

Part of the answer is of course the one with which we began, the evolution of moral orders through group selection: groups that behave in these ways simply survive and increase. But this cannot be the whole story. If not from an understanding of their beneficial effect in creating an as-yet unimaginable extended order of cooperation, whence did such rules of conduct originate? More important, how were they preserved against the strong opposition of instinct and, more recently, from the assaults of reason? Here we come to religion.

Custom and tradition, both non-rational adaptations to the environment, are more likely to guide group selection when supported by totem and taboo, or magical or religious beliefs – beliefs that themselves grew from the tendency to interpret any order men encountered in an animistic manner. At first the main function of such restraints on individual action may have been to serve as signs of recognition among members of the group. Later the belief in spirits that punished transgressors led such restraints to be preserved. 'The spirits are in general conceived as guardians of tradition. . . . Our ancestors live now as spirits in the other world. . . . They become angry and make things bad if we do not obey custom' (Malinowski, 1936:25).

But this is not yet sufficient for any real selection to occur, for such beliefs and the rites and ceremonies associated with them must also work on another level. Common practices must have a chance to produce their beneficial effects on a group on a progressive scale before selection by evolution can become effective. Meanwhile, how are they transmitted from generation to generation? Unlike genetic properties, cultural properties are not transmitted automatically. Transmission and non-transmission from generation to generation are as much positive or negative contributions to a stock of traditions as are any contributions by individuals. Many generations will therefore probably be required to ensure that any particular such traditions are indeed continued, and that they do indeed eventually spread. Mythical beliefs of some sort may be needed to bring this about, especially where rules of conduct conflicting with instinct are concerned. A merely utilitarian or even functionalist explanation of the different rites or ceremonies will be insufficient, and even implausible.

We owe it partly to mystical and religious beliefs, and, I believe, particularly to the main monotheistic ones, that beneficial traditions have been preserved and transmitted at least long enough to enable those groups following them to grow, and to have the opportunity to spread by natural or cultural selection. This means that, like it or not, we owe the persistence of certain practices, and the civilisation that resulted from them, in part to support from beliefs which are not true – or verifiable or testable – in the same sense as are scientific statements, and which are certainly not the result of rational argumentation. I sometimes think that it might be appropriate to call at least some of them, at least as a gesture of appreciation, 'symbolic truths', since they did help their adherents to 'be fruitful and multiply and replenish the earth and subdue it' (*Genesis* 1:28). Even those among us, like myself, who are not prepared to accept the anthropomorphic conception of a personal divinity ought to admit that the premature loss of what we regard as nonfactual beliefs would have deprived mankind of a powerful support in the long development of the extended order that we now enjoy, and that even now the loss of these beliefs, whether true or false, creates great difficulties.

In any case, the religious view that morals were determined by processes incomprehensible to us may at any rate be truer (even if not exactly in the way intended) than the rationalist delusion that man, by exercising his intelligence, invented morals that gave him the power to achieve more than he could ever foresee. If we bear these things in mind, we can better understand and appreciate those clerics who are said to have become somewhat sceptical of the validity of some of their teachings and who yet continued to teach them because they feared that a loss of faith would lead to a decline of morals. No doubt they were right; and even an agnostic ought to concede that we owe our morals, and the tradition that has provided not only our civilisation but our very lives, to the acceptance of such scientifically unacceptable factual claims.

The undoubted *historical* connection between religion and the values that have shaped and furthered our civilisation, such as the family and several property, does not of course mean that there is any *intrinsic* connection between religion as such and such values. Among the founders of religions over the last two thousand years, many opposed property and the family. *But the only religions that have survived are those which support property and the family.* Thus the outlook for communism, which is both anti-property and anti-family (and also anti-religion), is not promising. For it is, I believe, itself a religion which had its time, and which is now declining rapidly. In communist and socialist countries we are watching how the natural selection of religious beliefs disposes of the maladapted.

The decline of communism of which I speak is, of course, occurring mainly where it has actually been implemented – and has therefore been allowed to disappoint utopian hopes. It lives on, however, in the hearts of those who have not experienced its real effects: in Western intellectuals and among the poor on the periphery of the extended order, i.e., in the Third World. Among the former, there appears to be some growing sense that rationalism of the type criticised here is a false god; but the need for a god of some sort persists, and is met partly by such means as returning to a curious version of Hegelian dialectic which allows the illusion of rationality to coexist with a system of belief closed to criticism by unquestioned commitment to a 'humanist totality' (which, in fact, is itself supremely rationalistic in just the constructivist sense I have criticised). As Herbert Marcuse put it, 'Real freedom for individual existence (and not merely in the liberalist sense) is possible only in a specifically structured *polis*, a 'rationally' organized society' (quoted in Jay, 1973:119. To see what this 'rationality' means, see ibid., 49, 57, 60, 64, 81, 125, et passim). In the latter, 'liberation theology' may fuse with nationalism to produce a powerful new religion with disastrous consequences for people already in dire economic straits (see O'Brien, 1986).

How would religion have sustained beneficial customs? Customs whose beneficial effects were unperceivable by those practising them were likely to be preserved long enough to increase their selective advantage only when supported by some other strong beliefs; and some powerful supernatural or magic faiths were readily available to perform this role. As an order of human interaction became more extended, and still more threatening to instinctual claims, it might for a time become quite dependent on the continuing influence of some such religious beliefs – false reasons influencing men to do what was required to maintain the structure enabling them to nourish their enlarging numbers (see Appendix G).

But just as the very creation of the extended order was never intended, similarly there is no reason to suppose that the support derived from religion usually was deliberately cultivated, or that there was often anything 'conspiratorial' about all this. It is naive – particularly in light of our argument that we *cannot* observe the effects of our morals – to imagine some wise elite coolly calculating the effects of various morals, selecting among them, and conspiring to persuade the masses by Platonic 'noble lies' to swallow an 'opium of the people' and thus to obey what advanced the interests of their rulers. No doubt choice among particular versions of basic religious beliefs was often decided by expedient decisions of secular rulers. Moreover, religious support was, from time to time, deliberately, sometimes even cynically, enlisted by secular rulers; but frequently these would have concerned momentary disputes that hardly counted for much over long evolution-ary periods – periods wherein the question whether the favoured rule contributed to the increase of the community was more decisive than any question about what particular ruling clique may have coddled it during some particular period.

Some questions of language may also arise in describing and evaluating such developments. Ordinary language is inadequate to make the necessary distinctions sufficiently precise, especially where the concept of knowledge is concerned. For instance, is *knowledge* involved when a person has the habit of behaving in a manner that, without his knowing it, increases the likelihood that not only he and his family but also many others unknown to him will survive – particularly if he has preserved this habit for altogether different and indeed quite inaccurate grounds? Obviously what guided him successfully is not what is generally meant by rational knowledge. Nor is it helpful to describe such acquired practices as 'emotive' since they clearly are not always guided by what may legitimately be called emotions either, even though certain factors, such as fear of disapproval or punishment (whether human or divine), may often support or preserve particular habits. In many if not most cases, those who won through were those who stuck to 'blind habit' or learnt through religious teaching such things as that 'honesty is the best policy', thereby beating cleverer fellows who had 'reasoned' otherwise. As strategies for survival, counterparts of both rigidity and flexibility have played important roles in biological evolution; and morals that took the form of rigid rules may sometimes have been more effective than more flexible rules whose adherents attempted to steer their practice, and alter their course, according to particular facts and foreseeable consequences – and thus by something that it would be easier to call knowledge.

So far as I personally am concerned I had better state that I feel as little entitled to assert as to deny the existence of what others call God, for I must admit that I just do not know what this word is supposed to mean. I certainly reject every anthropomorphic, personal, or animistic interpretation of the term, interpretations through which many people succeed in giving it a meaning. The conception of a man-like or mind-like acting being appears to me rather the product of an arrogant overestimation of the capacities of a man-like mind. I cannot attach meaning to words that in the structure of my own thinking, or in my picture of the world, have no place that would give them meaning. It would thus be dishonest of me were I to use such words as if they expressed any belief that I hold.

I long hesitated whether to insert this personal note here, but ultimately decided to do so because support by a professed agnostic may help religious people more unhesitatingly to pursue those conclusions that we do share. Perhaps what many people mean in speaking of God is just a personification of that tradition of morals or values that keeps their community alive. The source of order that religion ascribes to a human-like divinity – the map or guide that will show a part successfully how to move within the whole – we now learn to see to be not outside the physical world but one of its characteristics, one far too complex for any of its parts possibly to form an 'image' or 'picture' of it. Thus religious prohibitions against idolatry, against the making of such images, are well taken. Yet perhaps most people can conceive of abstract tradition only as a personal Will. If so, will they not be inclined to find this will in 'society' in an age in which more overt supernaturalisms are ruled out as superstitions?

On that question may rest the survival of our civilisation.

APPENDICES

'NATURAL' VERSUS 'ARTIFICIAL'

Current scientific and philosophical usage is so deeply influenced by the Aristotelian tradition, which knows nothing of evolution, that existing dichotomies and contrasts not only usually fail to capture correctly the processes underlying the problems and conflicts discussed in chapter one, but actually hinder understanding of those problems and conflicts themselves. In this section I shall review some of these difficulties in classification, in the hope that some familiarity with the obstacles to understanding may in fact further understanding.

We may as well begin with the word 'natural', the source of much controversy and many misunderstandings. The original meaning of the Latin root of 'natural', as well as the Greek root of its equivalent 'physical', derive from verbs describing kinds of growth (*nascor* and *phyo* respectively; see Kerferd, 1981:111–150), so that it would be legitimate to describe as 'natural' anything that has grown spontaneously and not been deliberately designed by a mind. In this sense our traditional, spontaneously evolved morals are perfectly natural rather than artificial, and it would seem fitting to call such traditional rules 'natural law'.

But usage does not readily permit the understanding of natural law that I have just sketched. Rather, it tends to confine the word 'natural' to innate propensities or instincts that (as we saw in chapter one) often conflict with evolved rules of conduct. If such innate responses alone are described as 'natural', and if – to make matters worse – only what is necessary to preserve an existing state of affairs, particularly the order of the small group or immediate community, is described as 'good', we have to designate as both 'unnatural' and 'bad' even the first steps taken towards observing rules and thereby adapting to changing conditions – that is, the first steps towards civilisation.

Now if 'natural' must be used to mean innate or instinctual, and 'artificial' to mean the product of design, the results of cultural evolution (such as traditional rules) are clearly neither one nor the other – and thus are not only 'between instinct and reason', but also of course between 'natural' (i.e., instinctual) and 'artificial' (i.e., the product of reasonable design). The exclusive dichotomy of 'natural' and 'artificial', as well as the similar and related one of 'passion' and 'reason' – which, being exclusive, does not permit any area between these terms – has thus contributed greatly to the neglect and misunderstanding of the crucial exosomatic process of cultural evolution which produced the traditions that determined the growth of civilisation. In effect, these dichotomies define this area, and these processes, out of existence.

Yet if we go beyond these crude dichotomies, we see that the true opposite to passion is not reason but traditional morals. The evolution of a tradition of rules of conduct – standing *between* the processes of the evolution of instinct and those of reason – is a distinct process which it is quite mistaken to regard as a product of reason. Such traditional rules have indeed *grown* naturally in the course of evolution.

Growth is not an exclusive property of biological organisms. From the proverbial snowball to the deposits of wind or the formation of crystals – or waterborne sand, the rising of mountains and the formation of complex molecules – nature is full of examples of increase of size or structure. When we consider the emergence of structures of inter-relations among organisms, we find that it is also perfectly correct, etymologically and logically, to use the word 'growth' to describe them; and this is how I mean the word: namely, to designate a process occurring in a self-maintaining structure.

Thus to continue to contrast cultural with natural evolution leads back into the trap mentioned – the exclusive dichotomy between 'artificial' development guided by conscious design, and what is assumed to be 'natural' because it exhibits unchanging instinctual characteristics. Such interpretations of 'natural' easily force one in the direction of constructivist rationalism. Though constructivist interpre-tations are no doubt superior to organismic 'explanations' (now generally rejected as empty) that merely substitute one unexplained process for another, we should recognise that there are two distinct kinds of evolutionary process – both of which are perfectly natural processes. Cultural evolution, although a distinct process, remains in important respects more similar to genetic or biological evolution than to developments guided by reason or foreknowledge of the effects of decisions.

The similarity of the order of human interaction to that of biological organisms has of course often been noticed. But so long as we were unable to explain how the orderly structures of nature were formed, as long as we lacked an account of evolutionary selection, the analogies perceived were of limited help. With evolutionary selection, however, we are now supplied with a key to a general understanding of the formation of order in life, mind and interpersonal relations.

Incidentally, some of those orders, like that of the mind, may be capable of forming orders of a lower degree, yet are themselves not the products of orders of a higher level. This teaches us to recognise our limited power of explaining or designing an order belonging to a lower stage of the hierarchy of orders, as well as our inability to explain or design one of a higher order.

Having stated the general problem that interferes with clear usage of these traditional terms, we may as well indicate briefly, taking David Hume as an example, how even the thought of one of the most important thinkers in our tradition has been plagued by misunderstandings arising from such false dichotomies. Hume is a particularly good example since he unfortunately chose for the moral traditions that I would really prefer to call natural the term 'artificial' (probably borrowing from the common-law writers' expression 'artificial reason'). Ironically, this led to his being regarded as the founder of utilitarianism, despite his having stressed that 'though the rules of justice be *artificial* they are not arbitrary', and that therefore it is even not 'improper to call them laws of *nature*' (1739/1886:II,258). He endeavoured to safeguard himself against constructivistic misinterpretations by explaining that he 'only suppose[d] those reflections to be formed at once, which in fact arise insensibly and by degrees' (1739/1886:II,274). (Hume made use here of the device which Scottish moral philosophers called 'conjectural history' (Stewart, 1829:VII, 90, and Medick, 1973:134–176) – a device later often called 'rational reconstruction' – in a manner that may mislead and which his younger contemporary Adam Ferguson learnt systematically to avoid). As these passages suggest, Hume came close to an evolutionary interpretation, even perceiving that 'no form can persist unless it possesses those powers and organs necessary for its subsistence: some new order or economy must be tried and so on, without intermission; till at last some order which can support and maintain itself, is fallen upon'; and that man cannot 'pretend to an exemption from the lot of all living animals [because the] perpetual war among all living creatures' must go on (1779/1886:II, 429, 436). As has been well said, he practically recognised that 'there is a third category between natural and artificial which shares certain characteristics with both' (Haakonssen, 1981:24).

Yet the temptation to try to explain the function of self-organising structures by showing how such a structure might have been formed by a creating mind is great; and it is thus understandable that some of Hume's followers interpreted his term 'artificial' in this way, building on it a utilitarian theory of ethics according to which man consciously chooses his morals for their recognised utility.This may seem a curious view to ascribe to someone who had stressed that 'the rules of morality are not the conclusions of reason' (1739/1886:II, 235), but it was a misinterpretation that came naturally to a Cartesian rationalist such as C. V. Helvetius, from whom Jeremy Bentham admittedly derived his own constructions (see Everett, 1931:110).

Though in Hume, and also in the works of Bernard Mandeville, we can watch the gradual emergence of the twin concepts of the formations of spontaneous orders and of selective evolution (see Hayek, 1967/78:250, 1963/67:106–121 and 1967/78a:249–266), it was Adam Smith and Adam Ferguson who first made systematic use of this approach. Smith's work marks the breakthrough of an evolutionary approach which has progressively displaced the stationary Aristotelian view. The nineteenth-century enthusiast who claimed that the *Wealth of Nations* was in importance second only to the Bible has often been ridiculed; but he may not have exaggerated so much. Even Aristotle's disciple Thomas Aquinas could not conceal from himself that *multae utilitates impedirentur si omnia peccata districte prohiberentur* – that much that is useful would be prevented if all sins were strictly prohibited (*Summa Theologica*, II, ii, q. 78 i).

While Smith has been recognised by several writers as the originator of cybernetics (Emmet, 1958:90, Hardin, 1961:54), recent examinations of Charles Darwin's notebooks (Vorzimmer, 1977; Gruber, 1974) suggest that his reading of Adam Smith in the crucial year 1838 led Darwin to his decisive breakthrough.

Thus from the Scottish moral philosophers of the eighteenth century stem the chief impulses towards a theory of evolution, the variety of disciplines now known as cybernetics, general systems theory, synergetics, autopoiesis, etc., as well as the understanding of the superior self-ordering power of the market system, and of the evolution also of language, morals, and law (Ullman–Margalit, 1978, and Keller, 1982).

Adam Smith nevertheless remains the butt of jokes, even among economists, many of whom have not yet discovered that the analysis of self-ordering processes must be the chief task of any science of the market order. Another great economist, Carl Menger, a little more than a hundred years after Adam Smith, clearly perceived that 'this genetic element is inseparable from the conception of theoretical science' (Menger, 1883/1933:II,183, and cf. his earlier use of the term 'genetic' in Menger, 1871/1934:I,250). It was largely through such endeavors to understand the formation of human interaction through evolution and spontaneous formation of order that these approaches have become the main tools for dealing with such complex phenomena for the explanation of which 'mechanical laws' of one-directional causation are no longer adequate (see Appendix B).

In recent years the spreading of this evolutionary approach has so much affected the development of research that a report of the 1980 meeting of the *Gesellschaft Deutscher Naturforscher und Ärzte* could say that 'for modern science of nature a world of things and phenomena has become a world of structures and orders'.

Such recent advances in natural science have shown how right the American scholar Simon N. Patten was when, nearly ninety years ago, he wrote that 'just as Adam Smith was the last of the moralists and the first of the economists, so Darwin was the last of the economists and the first of the biologists' (1899, XXIII). Smith proves to have been even more than that: the paradigm he provided has since become a tool of great power in many branches of scientific effort.

Nothing better illustrates the humanistic derivation of the concept of evolution than that biology had to borrow its vocabulary from the humanities. The term 'genetic' that has now become perhaps the key technical term for the theory of biological evolution was apparently first used in its German form (*genetisch*) (Schulze, 1913:I, 242), in the writings of J. G. Herder (1767), Friedrich Schiller (1793) and C. M. Wieland (1800), long before Thomas Carlyle introduced it into English. It was used particularly in linguistics after Sir William Jones had in 1787 discovered the common descent of the Indo–European languages; and by the time that this had been elaborated in 1816 by Franz Bopp, the conception of cultural evolution had become a commonplace. We find the term used again in 1836 by Wilhelm von Humboldt (1977:III, 389 and 418), who in the same work also argued that 'if one conceived of the formation of language, as is most natural, as successsive, it becomes necessary to ascribe to it, as to all origin in nature, a system of evolution' (with thanks to Professor R. Keller, Düsseldorf, for this reference). Was it an accident that Humboldt was also a great advocate of individual freedom? And after the publication of Charles Darwin's work we find lawyers and linguists (aware of their kinship already in ancient Rome (Stein, 1966: chapter 3)), protest that they had been 'Darwinians before Darwin' (Hayek, 1973:153). It was not until after William Bateson's *Problems of Genetics* (1913) that 'genetics' rapidly became the distinctive name for biological evolution. Here we shall adhere to its modern use, established by Bateson, for biological inheritance through 'genes', to distinguish it from cultural inheritance through learning – which does not mean that the distinction can always be carried through precisely. The two forms of inheritance frequently interact, particularly by genetic inheritance determining what can or cannot be inherited by learning (i.e., culturally).

147

THE COMPLEXITY OF PROBLEMS OF HUMAN INTERACTION

Although physical scientists sometimes appear unwilling to recognise the greater complexity of the problems of human interaction, the fact itself was seen more than a hundred years ago by no less a figure than James Clerk Maxwell, who in 1877 wrote that the term 'physical science' is often applied 'in a more or less restricted manner to those branches of science in which the phenomena considered are of the simplest and most abstract kind, excluding the consideration of the more complex phenomena such as those observed in living things'. And more recently a Nobel laureate in physics, Louis W. Alvarez, stressed that 'actually physics is the simplest of all the sciences. . . . But in the case of an infinitely more complicated system, such as the population of a developing country like India, no one can yet decide how best to change the existing conditions' (Alvarez, 1968).

Mechanical methods and models of simple causal explanation are increasingly inapplicable as we advance to such complex phenomena. In particular, the crucial phenomena determining the formation of many highly complex structures of human interaction, i.e., economic values or prices, cannot be interpreted by simple causal or 'nomothetic' theories, but require explanation in terms of the joint effects of a larger number of distinct elements than we can ever hope individually to observe or manipulate.

It was only the 'marginal revolution' of the 1870s that produced a satisfactory explanation of the market processes that Adam Smith had long before described with his metaphor of the 'invisible hand', an account which, despite its still metaphorical and incomplete character, was the first scientific description of such self-ordering processes. James and John Stuart Mill, by contrast, were unable to conceive of the determination of market values in any manner other than causal determination by a few preceding events, and this inability barred them, as it does many modern 'physicalists', from understanding self-steering market processes. An understanding of the truths underlying marginal utility theory was further delayed by James Mill's guiding influence on David Ricardo, as well as by Karl Marx's own work. Attempts to achieve mono-causal explanations in such areas (prolonged even longer in England through the decisive influence of Alfred Marshall and his school) persist to the present.

John Stuart Mill perhaps played the most important role in this connection. He had early put himself under socialist influence, and through this bias acquired a great appeal to 'progressive' intellectuals, establishing a reputation as the leading liberal and the 'Saint of Rationalism'. Yet he probably led more intellectuals into socialism than any other single person: fabianism was in its beginnings essentially formed by a group of his followers.

Mill had barred his way to comprehending the guide function of prices by his doctrinaire assurance that 'there is nothing in the laws of value which remains for the present or any future writer to clear up' (1848/1965, *Works*: III, 456), an assurance that made him believe that 'considerations of value had to do with [the distribution of wealth] alone' and not with its production (1848/1965, *Works*, III: 455). Mill was blinded to the function of prices by his assumption that only a process of mechanical causation by some few observable preceding events constituted a legitimate explanation in terms of the standards of natural science. Due to the influence that Mill's assumption had exerted for so long, the 'marginal revolution' of twenty-five years later, when it did arrive, had an explosive effect.

It deserves mentioning here, however, that only six years after Mill's textbook was published, H. H. Gossen, a thinker who is almost wholly overlooked, had anticipated marginal utility theory in already clearly recognising the dependence of extended production on guidance by prices and emphasising that 'only with the establishment of private property can the yardstick be found for the determination of the optimal quantity of each commodity to be produced under given circumstances. . . . The greatest possible protection of private property is definitely the greatest necessity for the continuation of human society' (1854/1983:254–5).

Despite the great harm done by his work, we must probably forgive Mill much for his infatuation with the lady who later became his wife – upon whose death, in his opinion, 'this country lost the greatest mind it contained' and who, according to his testimony, 'in the nobleness of her public object . . . never stopped short of perfect distributive justice as the final aim, implying therefore a state of society entirely communist in practice and spirit' (1965, *Works*: XV, 601; and see Hayek, 1951).

Whatever the influence of Mill may be, Marxian economics is still today attempting to explain highly complex orders of interaction in terms of single causal effects like mechanical phenomena rather than as prototypes of those self-ordering processes which give us access to the explanation of highly complex phenomena. It deserves mention however that, as Joachim Reig has pointed out (in his Introduction to the Spanish translation of E. von Böhm–Bawerk's essay on Marx's theory of exploitation (1976)), it would seem that after learning of the works of Jevons and Menger, Karl Marx himself completely abandoned further work on capital. If so, his followers were evidently not so wise as he.

TIME AND THE EMERGENCE AND REPLICATION OF STRUCTURES

The fact that certain structures can form and multiply because other similar structures that already exist can transmit their properties to others (subject to occasional variations), and that abstract orders can thus undergo a process of evolution in the course of which they pass from one material embodiment into others that will arise only because the pattern already exists, has given our world a new dimension: time's arrow (Blum, 1951). In the course of time new features arise which did not exist before: self-perpetuating and evolving structures which, though represented at any one moment only by particular material embodiments, become distinct entities that in various manifestations persist through time.

The possibility of forming structures by a process of replication gives those elements that have the capacity for doing so better chances of multiplying. Those elements will be preferably selected for multiplication that are capable of forming into more complex structures, and the increase of their members will lead to the formation of still more such structures. Such a model, once it has appeared, becomes as definite a constituent of the order of the world as any material object. In the structures of interaction, the patterns of activities of groups are determined by practices transmitted by individuals of one generation to those of the next; and these orders preserve their general character only by constant change (adaptation).

ALIENATION, DROPOUTS, AND THE CLAIMS OF PARASITES

In this section I should like to record a few reflections about the matters named in the title of this section.

1. As we have seen, conflict between an individual's emotions and what is expected of him in an extended order is virtually inevitable: innate responses tend to break through the network of learnt rules that maintain civilisation. But only Rousseau provided literary and intellectual credentials for reactions that cultivated people once dismissed as simply uncouth. Regarding the natural (read 'instinctual') as good or desirable is, in his work, an expression of nostalgia for the simple, the primitive, or even the barbarian, based on the conviction that one ought to satisfy his or her desires, rather than to obey shackles allegedly invented and imposed by selfish interests.

In a milder form, disappointment at the failure of our traditional morality to produce greater pleasure has recently found expression in nostalgia for the small that is beautiful, or in complaints about *The Joyless Economy* (Schumacher, 1973, Scitovsky, 1976, as well as much of the literature of 'alienation').

2. Mere existence cannot confer a right or moral claim on anyone against any other. Persons or groups may incur duties to particular individuals; but as part of the system of common rules that assist humankind to grow and multiply not even all existing lives have a moral claim to preservation. A practice that seems so harsh to us wherein some Eskimo tribes leave senile members to die at the beginning of their seasonal migration may well be necessary for them to bring their offspring to the next season. And it is at least an open question whether it is a moral duty to prolong the lives of suffering incurables as long as modern medicine can. Such questions arise even before we ask to whom such claims can be validly addressed.

Rights derive from systems of relations of which the claimant has become a part through helping to maintain them. If he ceases to do so, or has never done so (or nobody has done so for him) there exists no ground on which such claims could be founded. Relations between individuals can exist only as products of their wills, but the mere wish of a claimant can hardly create a duty for others. Only expectations produced by long practice can create duties for the members of the community in which they prevail, which is one reason why prudence must be exercised in the creation of expectations, lest one incur a duty that one cannot fulfill.

3. Socialism has taught many people that they possess claims irrespective of performance, irrespective of participation. In the light of the morals that produced the extended order of civilisation, socialists in fact incite people to break the law.

Those who claim to have been 'alienated' from what most of them apparently never learnt, and who prefer to live as parasitic dropouts, draining the products of a process to which they refuse to contribute, are true followers of Rousseau's appeal for a return to nature, representing as the chief evil those institutions that made possible the formation of an order of human coordination.

I do not question any individual's right voluntarily to withdraw from civilisation. But what 'entitlements' do such persons have? Are we to subsidise their hermitages? There cannot be any entitlement to be exempted from the rules on which civilisation rests. We may be able to assist the weak and disabled, the very young and old, but only if the sane and adult submit to the impersonal discipline which gives us means to do so.

It would be quite wrong to regard such errors as originating with the young. They reflect what they are taught, the pronouncements of their parents – and of departments of psychology and sociology of education and the characteristic intellectuals whom they produce – pale reproductions of Rousseau and Marx, Freud and Keynes, transmitted through intellects whose desires have outrun their understanding.

PLAY, THE SCHOOL OF RULES

The practices that led to the formation of the spontaneous order have much in common with rules observed in playing a game. To attempt to trace the origin of competition in play would lead us too far astray, but we can learn much from the masterly and revealing analysis of the role of play in the evolution of culture by the historian Johan Huizinga, whose work has been insufficiently appreciated by students of human order (1949: esp. 5, 11, 24, 47, 51, 59, and 100, and see Knight, 1923/1936:46, 50, 60–66; and Hayek, 1976:71 and n. 10).

Huizinga writes that 'in myth and ritual the great instinctive forces of civilised life have their origin: law and order, commerce and profit, craft and art, poetry, wisdom and science. All are rooted in the primaeval soil of play' (1949:5); play 'creates order, is order' (1950:10). . . . 'It proceeds within its own proper boundaries of time and space according to fixed rules and in an orderly manner' (1949:15 and 51).

A game is indeed a clear instance of a process wherein obedience to common rules by elements pursuing different and even conflicting purposes results in overall order. Modern game theory has, moreover, shown that while some games lead to the gains of one side being evenly balanced by the gains of the other, other games may produce overall net gain. The growth of the extended structure of interaction was made possible by the individual's entry into the latter sorts of game, ones leading to overall increase of productivity.

REMARKS ON THE ECONOMICS AND ANTHROPOLOGY OF POPULATION

The matters discussed in chapter eight have concerned economics from its origins. The science of economics may well be said to have begun in 1681, when Sir William Petty (a slightly older colleague of Sir Isaac Newton, and among the founders of the Royal Society) became fascinated by the causes of the rapid growth of London. To everybody's surprise he found that it had grown bigger than Paris and Rome together, and in an essay on *The Growth, Increase and Multiplication of Mankind* he explained how greater density of population made a greater division of labour possible:

> Each manufacture will be divided in as many parts as possible. In the making of a watch, if one man shall make the wheels, another the spring, another shall engrave the dial plate, then the watch will be better and cheaper than if the same work were put on any one man.
>
> And we also see that in towns and in the streets of great towns, where all the inhabitants are almost of one trade, the commodity peculiar to those places is made better and cheaper than elsewhere. Moreover, when all sorts of manufacture are made in one place, there every ship that goes forth can suddenly have its loading of so many particulars and species as the port whereunto she is bound can take off (1681/1899:II, 453 and 473).

Petty also recognised that 'fewness of people, is real poverty; and a Nation wherein are Eight Millions of people are more than twice as rich as the same scope of land wherein are but four; For the Governors which are the great charge, may serve near as well for the greater as the lesser number' (1681/1899:II, 454–55, and 1927:II, 48). Unfortunately, the special essay he wrote on 'The Multiplication of Mankind' appears to be lost (1681/1899:I, 454–55 and 1927:I, 43), but it is evident that the general conception was transmitted from him through Bernard Mandeville (1715/1924:I, 356) to Adam Smith, who noticed, as remarked in chapter eight, that division of labour is limited by the extent of the market, and that population increase is crucial to the prosperity of a country.

If economists have from an early date been preoccupied with such questions, anthropologists in recent times have given insufficient attention to the evolution of morals (which of course can scarcely ever be 'observed'); and not only the crudities of social Darwinism but also socialist prejudices have discouraged the pursuit of evolutionary approaches. Nevertheless we find an eminent socialist anthropologist, in a study of 'Urban Revolution', define 'revolution' as 'the culmination of the progressive change in the economic structure and social organisation of communities that caused, or was accompanied by, a dramatic increase of the population affected' (Childe, 1950:3). Important insights are also found in the writings of M. J. Herskovits, who states:

> The relation of population size to environment and technology on the one hand, and to per capita production on the other, offers the greatest challenge in investigating the combinations which make for an economic surplus among a given people. . . .
>
> On the whole it seems that the problem of survival is most pressing in the smallest societies. Conversely, it is among the larger groups, where the specialisation appears which is essential in providing more goods than are sufficient to support all people, that the enjoyment of social leisure is made possible (1960:398).

What is often represented by biologists (e.g., Carr–Saunders, 1922, Wynne–Edwards, 1962, Thorpe, 1976) as primarily a mechanism for limiting population might equally well be described as a mechanism for increasing, or better for adapting, numbers to a long-run equilibrium to the supporting power of the territory, taking as much advantage of new possibilities to maintain larger numbers as of any damage which a temporary excess might cause. Nature is as inventive in the one respect as in the other, and the human brain was probably the most successful structure enabling one species to outgrow all others in power and extent.

SUPERSTITION AND THE PRESERVATION OF TRADITION

This volume was nearly ready for the printers when a friendly comment by Dr. D. A. Rees on a lecture I had given drew my attention to a remarkable little study by Sir James Frazer (1909) – *Psyche's Task* – bearing the subtitle given above. In it, as Frazer explained, he endeavoured to 'sort out the seeds of good from the seeds of evil'. It deals with my central subject in a manner in many respects similar, but, coming as it does from a distinguished anthropologist, it is able to give, particularly on the early development of property and the family, so much more empirical evidence that I wish I could reprint the whole of its 84 pages as an illustrative appendix to this volume. Among those of his conclusions which are pertinent to this volume, he explains how superstition, by strengthening respect for marriage, contributed to stricter observance of rules of sexual morality among both married and unmarried. In his chapter on private property (17), Frazer points out that 'the effect of tabooing a thing [was] to endow it with a supernatural or magical energy that rendered it practically unapproachable by any but the owner. Thus taboo became a powerful instrument for strengthening the ties, perhaps our socialist friends would say riveting the chains, of private property'. And later (19), he quotes a much earlier author who reports that in New Zealand a 'form of *tapu* was a great preserver of property', and an even earlier report (20) about the Marquand Islands where 'without doubt the first mission of taboo was to establish property the basis of all society'.

Frazer also concluded (82) that 'superstition rendered a great service to humanity. It supplied multitudes with a motive, a wrong motive it is true, for right action; and surely it is better for the world that men should be right from wrong motives than that they would do wrong with the best intentions. What concerns society is conduct, not opinion: if only our actions are just and good, it matters not a straw to others whether our opinions are mistaken'.

EDITOR'S ACKNOWLEDGEMENTS

The Editor expresses his gratitude, above all, to Professor Hayek's assistant, Miss Charlotte Cubitt, for her exceptional help in preparing this manuscript for publication. He also wishes to thank his own research assistants, Timothy Brien, Timothy Groseclose, Kenneth Rock, Kristen Moynihan, and Leif Wenar, of Stanford University, for their work on the text; and his colleagues Dr. Mikhail Bernstam, The Hoover Institution, Mr. Jeffrey Friedman, University of California, Berkeley, Dr. Hannes Gissurarson, University of Iceland, Dr. Robert Hessen, The Hoover Institution, Ms. Gene Opton, Berkeley, Professor Gerard Radnitzky, University of Trier, Professor Julian Simon, University of Maryland, and Professor Robert G. Wesson, The Hoover Institution, for their careful reading of the manuscript and helpful suggestions. They are of course not responsible for any errors that remain.

W. W. Bartley, III
Stanford, California
May 1987

BIBLIOGRAPHY

Alchian, Armen (1950), 'Uncertainty, Evolution and Economic Theory', *Journal of Political Economy 58*, reprinted in revised form in Alchian (1977).

Alchian, Armen (1977), *Economic Forces at Work* (Indianapolis: Liberty Press).

Alland, A., Jr. (1967), *Evolution and Human Behavior* (New York: Natural History Press).

Alvarez, Louis W. (1968), 'Address to Students', in *Les Prix Nobel*.

Babbage, Charles (1832), *On the Economy of Machinery and Manufacture* (London: C. Knight).

Baechler, Jean (1975), *The Origin of Capitalism* (Oxford: Blackwell).

Bailey, S. (1840), *A Defence of Joint-Stock Banks and Country Issues* (London: James Ridgeway).

Barker, Ernest (1948), *Traditions of Civility* (Cambridge: Cambridge University Press).

Barry, Brian M. (1961), 'Justice and the Common Good', *Analysis 19*.

Bartley, W. W., III (1962/84), *The Retreat to Commitment* (New York: Alfred A. Knopf, Inc., 1962), 2nd, revised and enlarged edition (La Salle: Open Court, 1984).

Bartley, W. W., III (1964), 'Rationality versus the Theory of Rationality', in Mario Bunge, ed.: *The Critical Approach to Science and Philosophy* (New York: The Free Press).

Bartley, W. W., III (1978), 'Consciousness and Physics: Quantum Mechanics, Probability, Indeterminism, the Body-Mind Problem', in *Philosophia*, 1978, pp. 675–716.

Bartley, W. W., III (1982), 'Rationality, Criticism and Logic', *Philosophia*, 1982, pp. 121–221.

Bartley, W. W., III (1985/87), 'Knowledge Is Not a Product Fully Known to Its Producer', in Kurt R. Leube and Albert Zlabinger, eds., *The Political Economy of Freedom* (Munich: Philosophia Verlag, 1985); and in revised and expanded form as 'Alienated Alienated: The Economics of Knowledge versus the Psychology and Sociology of Knowledge', in Radnitzky and Bartley (1987).

Bateson, William (1913), *Problems of Genetics* (New Haven: Yale University Press).

159

Bauer, Peter (1957), *Economic Analysis and Policy in Underdeveloped Countries* (London: Cambridge University Press).

Bauer, Peter (1971), 'Economic History as a Theory', *Economica N.S. 38*, pp. 163–179.

Bauer, Peter (1972), *Dissent on Development* (Cambridge, Mass.: Harvard University Press).

Bauer, Peter (1981), *Equality. The Third World and Economic Delusions* (Cambridge, Mass.: Harvard University Press).

Bauer, Peter and Basil S. Yamey (1957), *The Economics of Underdeveloped Countries* (Chicago: University of Chicago Press).

Baumgardt, D. (1952), *Bentham and the Ethics of Today* (Princeton: Princeton University Press).

Bell, Daniel and Irving Kristol, eds. (1971), *Capitalism Today* (New York: Basic Books, Inc.).

Bentham, Jeremy (1789/1887), *Works*, ed. John Bowring (Edinburgh: W. Tait).

Bloch, Ernst (1954–59), *Das Prinzip Hoffnung* (Berlin: Aufbau Verlag; English translation, *The Principle of Hope* (Cambridge, Mass.: MIT Press, 1986)).

Blum, H. F. (1951), *Time's Arrow and Evolution* (Princeton: Princeton University Press).

Bonner, John Tyler (1980), *The Evolution of Culture in Animals* (Princeton: Princeton University Press).

Bopp, F. (1927), *Geschichte der indogermanischen Sprachwissenschaft* (Berlin: Grundriß der indogermanischen Sprach-und Altertumskunde).

Born, Max (1968), *My Life and My Views* (New York: C. Scribner).

Boserup, Esther (1965), *The Conditions of Agricultural Growth* (London: George Allen & Unwin).

Boserup, Esther (1981), *Population and Technological Change. A Study of Long Term Trends* (Chicago: University of Chicago Press).

Braudel, Fernand (1981), *Civilization and Capitalism: 15th-18th Century*, Vol. I, *The Structures of Everyday Life: The Limits of the Possible* (New York: Harper & Row).

Braudel, Fernand (1982a), *Civilization and Capitalism: 15th-18th Century*, Vol. II, *The Wheels of Commerce* (New York: Harper & Row).

Braudel, Fernand (1982b), in *Le Monde*, March 16.

Braudel, F. (1984), *Civilization and Capitalism: 15th-18th Century*, Vol. III, *The Perspective of the World* (New York: Harper & Row).

Bullock, Allan and Oliver Stallybrass, eds. (1977), *The Harper Dictionary of Modern Thought* (New York: Harper & Row). Published in Britain as *The Fontana Dictionary of Modern Thought*.

Burke, E. P. (1816), 'Letter to a Member of the National Assembly', in *Works* (London: F. C. & J. Rivington).

Butler, Samuel (1663–1678), *Hudibras*, Part I (London: J. G. for Richard Marriot under Saint Dunstan's Church in Fleet Street, 1663); Part II (London: T. R. for John Martyn and James Allestry at the Bell in St. Paul's Church Yard, 1664); Part III (London: Simon Miller at the Sign of the Star at the West End of St. Paul's, 1678).

Campbell, B. G., ed. (1972), *Sexual Selection and the Descent of Man, 1871–1971* (Chicago: Aldine Publishing Co.).

Campbell, Donald T. (1974), 'Evolutionary Epistemology', in P. A. Schilpp, ed.: *The Philosophy of Karl Popper* (La Salle: Open Court, 1974), pp. 413–463, reprinted in Radnitzky and Bartley (1987).

Campbell, Donald T. (1977), 'Descriptive Epistemology', William James Lectures, Harvard University, mimeographed.

Carlyle, Thomas (1909), *Past and Present* (Oxford: Oxford University Press).

Carr–Saunders, A. M. (1922), *The Population Problem: A Study in Human Evolution* (Oxford: Clarendon Press).

Chagnon, Napoleon A. and William Irons, eds. (1979), *Evolutionary Biology and Human Social Behaviour* (North Scituate, Mass.: Duxbury Press).

Chapman, J. W. (1964), 'Justice and Fairness', *Nomos 6, Justice* (New York: New York University Press).

Childe, V. Gordon (1936), *Man Makes Himself* (New York: Oxford University Press).

Childe, V. Gordon (1936/81), *Man Makes Himself*, Introduction by Sally Green (Bradford-on-Avon, Wiltshire: Moonraker, 1981).

Childe, V. Gordon (1950), 'The Urban Revolution', *The Town Planning Report*.

Clark, Grahame (1965), 'Traffic in Stone Axe and Adze Blades', *Economic History Review 18*, 1965, pp. 1–28.

Clark, R. W. (1971), *Einstein: The Life and Times* (New York: World Publishing Company).

Clifford, W. K. (1879), 'On the Scientific Basis of Morals' (1875) and 'Right and Wrong: the Scientific Ground of their Distinction' (1876), in *Lectures and Essays*, Vol. 2 (London: Macmillan & Co.).

Coase, R. H. (1937), 'The Nature of the Firm', *Economica 4*.

Coase, R. H. (1960), 'The Problem of Social Cost', *Journal of Law and Economics 3*.

Coase, R. H. (1976), 'Adam Smith's View of Man', *Journal of Law and Economics*.

Cohen, J. E. (1984), 'Demographic Doomsday Deferred', *Harvard Magazine*.

Cohen, Morris R. (1931), *Reason and Nature* (New York: Harcourt, Brace and Co.).

Cohn, Norman (1970), *The Pursuit of the Millennium*, revised and expanded edition (New York: Oxford University Press).

Comte, A. (1854), 'La superiorité neçessaire de la morale demontrée sur la morale revelée', in *Système de la politique positive, I* (Paris: L. Mathias), p. 356.

Confucius, *Analects*, trans. A. Waley (London: George Allen & Unwin, Ltd., 1938).

Curran, Charles (1958), *The Spectator*, July 6, p. 8.

Dairaines, Serge (1934), *Un Socialisme d'Etat quinze Siècles avant Jesus-Christ* (Paris: Libraire Orientaliste P. Geuthner).

Demandt, Alexander (1978), *Metaphern für Geschichte*, (Munich: Beck).

Durham, William (1979), 'Towards a Co-evolutionary Theory of Human Biology and Culture', in N. Chagnon and W. Irons, eds., *Evolutionary Biology and Human Social Behaviour* (North Scituate, Mass.: Duxbury Press).

Edelman, Gerald M. (1987), *Neural Darwinism: The Theory of Neuronal Group Selection* (New York: Basic Books).

Edmonds, J. M. (1959), *The Fragments of Attic Comedy*, Vol. II (Leiden: E. J. Brill), in three volumes 1957–61.

Einaudi, Luigi (1948), 'Greatness and Decline of Planned Economy in the Hellenistic World', *Kyklos II*, pp. 193–210, 289–316.

Einstein, A. (1949/56), 'Why Socialism?', in *Out of My Later Years* (New York: Philosophical Library); see also *Monthly Review*, May 1949.

Emmet, Dorothy M. (1958), *Function, Purpose and Powers: Some Concepts in the Study of Individuals and Societies* (London: Macmillan).

Evans–Pritchard, E. (1965), *Theories of Primitive Religion* (Oxford: Clarendon Press).

Everett, C. W. (1931), *The Education of Jeremy Bentham* (New York: Columbia University Press).

Farb, Peter (1968), *Man's Rise to Civilization* (New York: Dutton).

Farb, Peter (1978), *Humankind* (Boston: Houghton Mifflin).

Ferguson, Adam (1767/1773), *An Essay on the History of Civil Society*, third edition (London: A. Millar and T. Caddel).

Ferguson, Adam (1792), *Principles of Moral and Political Science*, Vol. II (Edinburgh: A. Strahan and T. Caddel).

Ferri, Enrico (1895), *Annales de l'Institut Internationale de Sociologie I.*

Finley, Moses I. (1973), *An Ancient Economy* (London: Chatto and Windus, Ltd.).

Flew, A. G. N. (1967), *Evolutionary Ethics* (London: Macmillan).

Fontana/Harper Dictionary of Modern Thought (1977), see Bullock and Stallybrass.

Frazer, J. G. (1909), *Psyche's Task* (London: Macmillan).

Freud, Sigmund (1930), *Civilization and Its Discontents* (London: Hogarth Press).

Ghiselin, Michael T. (1969), *The Triumph of the Darwinian Method* (Berkeley: University of California Press).

Gossen, H. H. (1854/1889/1927/1983), *Entwicklung der Gesetze des menschlichen Verkehrs und der daraus fließenden Regeln für menschliches Handeln* (Braunschweig: Vieweg, 1854; Berlin: R. L. Prager, 1889; third edition, with introduction by F. A. Hayek (Berlin: R. L. Prager, 1927); English translation: *The Laws of Human Relations and the Rules of Human Action Derived Therefrom*, trans. Rudolph C. Blitz (Cambridge: MIT Press, 1983)).

Gruber, Howard E. (1974), *Darwin on Man: A Psychological Study of Scientific Creativity, together with Darwin's Early and Unpublished Notebooks*, transcribed and annotated by Paul H. Barrett (New York: E. P. Dutton & Co., Inc.).

Haakonssen, Knud (1981), *The Science of a Legislator: the Natural Jurisprudence of David Hume and Adam Smith* (Cambridge: Cambridge University Press).

Hardin, Garrett James (1961), *Nature and Man's Fate* (New York: The New American Library).

Hardin, Garrett James (1980), *Promethean Ethics: Living with Death, Competition and Triage* (St. Louis: Washington University Press).

Hardy, Alister (1965), *The Living Stream: Evolution and Man* (New York: Harper & Row).

Hayek, F. A. (1935), ed., *Collectivist Economic Planning: Critical Studies on the Possibilities of Socialism* (London: George Routledge & Sons).

Hayek, F. A. (1936/48), 'Economics and Knowledge', reprinted in Hayek (1948).

Hayek, F. A. (1941), *The Pure Theory of Capital* (London: Routledge & Kegan Paul, Ltd.).

Hayek, F. A. (1945/48), 'The Use of Knowledge in Society', reprinted in Hayek (1948).

Hayek, F. A. (1948), *Individualism and Economic Order* (London: Routledge & Kegan Paul, Ltd.).

Hayek, F. A. (1949/67), 'The Intellectuals and Socialism', *University of Chicago Law Review 16*, Spring 1949; reprinted in Hayek (1967).

Hayek, F. A. (1951), *John Stuart Mill and Harriet Taylor: Their Friendship and Subsequent Marriage* (London: Routledge & Kegan Paul).

Hayek, F. A. (1952), *The Sensory Order* (Chicago: University of Chicago Press).

Hayek, F. A. (1952/79), *The Counter-Revolution of Science: Studies on the Abuse of Reason* (Indianapolis: Liberty Press, 1979).

Hayek, F. A. (1954/1967), 'History and Politics', in F. A. Hayek, ed., *Capitalism and the Historians* (London: Routledge & Kegan Paul, Ltd., 1954), reprinted in Hayek (1967).

Hayek, F. A. (1960), *The Constitution of Liberty* (London: Routledge &

163

Kegan Paul, Ltd.).

Hayek, F. A. (1963/67), 'The Legal and Political Philosophy of David Hume', *Il Politico*, XXVIII/4, reprinted in Hayek (1967).

Hayek, F. A. (1964) 'The Theory of Complex Phenomena', in Mario A. Bunge, ed., *The Critical Approach to Science and Philosophy: Essays in Honor of Karl R. Popper* (New York: Free Press, 1964), reprinted in Hayek (1967).

Hayek, F. A. (1967), *Studies in Philosophy, Politics and Economics* (London: Routledge & Kegan Paul, Ltd.).

Hayek, F. A. (1967/78a), 'Dr. Bernard Mandeville', in *Proceedings of the British Academy*, *52*, reprinted in Hayek (1978).

Hayek, F. A. (1967/78b), 'The Confusion of Language in Political Thought', address delivered in German to the Walter Eucken Institute in Freiburg im Breisgau and published in 1968 as an Occasional Paper by the Institute of Economic Affairs, London; reprinted in Hayek (1978).

Hayek, F. A. (1970/78), *Die Irrtümer des Konstruktivismus und die Grundlagen legitimer Kritik gesellschaftlicher Gebilde* (Munich and Salzburg: Fink Verlag, 1970), reprinted (Tübingen: J. C. B. Mohr (Paul Siebeck) Verlag, 1975), published in English translation in Hayek (1978).

Hayek, F. A. (1972/78), *A Tiger by the Tail* (London: Institute of Economic Affairs).

Hayek, F. A. (1973), *Law, Legislation and Liberty*, Vol. I, *Rules and Order* (London: Routledge & Kegan Paul, Ltd.).

Hayek, F. A. (1976), *Law, Legislation and Liberty*, Vol. II, *The Mirage of Social Justice* (London: Routledge & Kegan Paul, Ltd.).

Hayek, F. A. (1976/78), *Denationalisation of Money* (London: The Institute of Economic Affairs, second edition, revised and expanded, 1978).

Hayek, F. A. (1978), *New Studies in Philosophy, Politics, Economics and the History of Ideas* (London: Routledge & Kegan Paul, Ltd.).

Hayek, F. A. (1979): *Law, Legislation and Liberty*, Vol. III, *The Political Order of a Free People* (London: Routledge & Kegan Paul, Ltd.).

Hayek, F. A. (1983), 'The Weasel Word "Social" ', *Salisbury Review*, Autumn 1983.

Hayek, F. A. (1986), 'Market Standards for Money', *Economic Affairs*, April/May, pp. 8–10.

Heilbroner, Robert (1970), *Between Capitalism and Socialism: Essays in Political Economics* (New York: Random House).

Herder, J. G. (1784/1821), *Ideen zur Philosophie der Geschichte der Menschheit* (Leipzig: J. F. Hartknoch, second ed., 1821). See also *Abhandlung über den Ursprung der Sprache*, 1772.

Herskovits, M. J. (1948), *Man and His Works* (New York: Alfred A. Knopf, Inc.).

Herskovits, M. J. (1960), *Economic Anthropology, A Study in Comparative Economics* (New York: Alfred A. Knopf, Inc.).

Hirschmann, Albert O. (1977), *The Passions and the Interests: Political Arguments for Capitalism Before Its Triumph* (Princeton: Princeton University Press).

Hobhouse, L. T. (1911), *Liberalism* (New York: Henry Holt & Co.).

Hobhouse, L. T. (1922), *The Elements of Social Justice* (New York: Henry Holt & Co.).

Holdsworth, W. S. (1924), *A History of English Law* (London: Methuen).

Howard, J. H. (1982), *Darwin* (Oxford: Oxford University Press).

Huizinga, Johan (1949), *Homo Ludens. A Study of the Play Element in Culture* (London: Routledge & Kegan Paul).

Humboldt, Wilhelm von (1836/1903), *Über die Verschiedenheit des menschlichen Sprachbaues und ihren Einfluss auf die geistige Entwicklung des Menschengeschlechtes* (Berlin: Druckerei der Königlichen Akademie der Wissenschaften), reprinted in *Gesammelte Schriften*, VII/1 (Berlin: B. Behr, 1903–36).

Humboldt, Wilhelm von (1903–36), *Gesammelte Schriften* (Berlin: B. Behr); also (Darmstadt, 1977), eds. A. Flitner and K. Giel.

Hume, David (c1757/1779/1886), *Dialogues concerning Natural Religion*, in David Hume, *Philosophical Works*, Vol. II., ed. T. H. Green and T. H. Grose (London: Longmans, Green).

Hume, David (1777/1886), *Enquiry Concerning Human Understanding*, in David Hume, *Philosophical Works*, Vol. III, ed. T. H. Green and T. H. Grose (London: Longmans, Green).

Hume, David (1741, 1742, 1758, 1777/1886), *Essays, Moral, Political and Literary*, in David Hume, *Philosophical Works*, Vols. III and IV, ed. T. H. Green and T. H. Grose (London: Longmans, Green).

Hume, David (1762), *History of England from the Invasion of Julius Caesar to the Revolution of 1688*, in six volumes (London: Printed for A. Millar in the Strand).

Hume, David (1882), *The Philosophical Works of David Hume*, eds. T. H. Green & T. H. Grose (London: Longmans, Green).

Hume, David (1739/1886), *A Treatise of Human Nature*, in David Hume, *Philosophical Works*, Vols. I and II, ed. T. H. Green and T. H. Grose (London: Longmans, Green).

Huxley, Julian S. and Thomas Henry Huxley (1947), *Touchstone for Ethics, 1893–1943* (New York: Harper).

Jay, Martin (1973), *The Dialectical Imagination* (Boston: Little, Brown).

Jones, E. L. (1981), *The European Miracle* (Cambridge: Cambridge University Press).

Jouvenel, Bertrand de (1957), *Sovereignty: An Inquiry into the Political Good,* translated by J. F. Huntington (Chicago: University of Chicago Press).

Kant, Immanuel (1798), *Der Streit der Fakultäten.*

Keller, R. (1982), 'Zur Theorie sprachlichen Wandels', *Zeitschrift für Germanistische Linguistik 10,* 1982, pp. 1–27.

Kerferd, G. B. (1981), *The Sophistic Movement* (Cambridge: Cambridge University Press), esp. Chapter 10: 'The nomos-physis Controversy'.

Keynes, J. M. (1923/71), *A Tract on Monetary Reform,* reprinted in *Collected Works* (London: Macmillan, 1971), IV.

Keynes, J. M. (1938/49/72), 'My Early Beliefs', written in 1938, printed in *Two Memoirs* (London: Rupert Hart–David, 1949), and reprinted in *Collected Works,* Vol. X (London: MacMillan, 1972).

Kirsch, G. (1981), 'Ordnungspolitik mir graut vor dir', *Frankfurter Allgemeine Zeitung,* 18 July 1981.

Knight, Frank H. (1923/36), *The Ethics of Competition and Other Essays* (London: G. Allen & Unwin, Ltd., 1936); *Quarterly Journal of Economics,* 1923.

Leakey, R. E. (1981), *The Making of Mankind* (New York: Dutton).

Liddell, H. G. and R. Scott (1940), *A Greek–English Lexicon,* 9th edition (London: Clarendon Press).

Locke, John (1676/1954), *Essays on the Laws of Nature,* ed. W. Leyden (Oxford: Clarendon Press).

Locke, John (1690/1887), *Two Treatises on Civil Government,* 2nd edition (London: Routledge).

Locke, John (1690/1924), *Essay Concerning Human Understanding,* ed. A. S. Pringle–Pattison (Oxford: Clarendon Press).

Machlup, Fritz (1962), *The Production and Distribution of Knowledge* (Princeton: Princeton University Press).

Maier, H. (1972), 'Können Begriffe die Gesellschaft verändern?', in *Sprache und Politik, Bergedorfer Gesprächkreis 41, Tagung,* May 1972 Protokoll.

Maine, H. S. (1875), *Lectures on the Early History of Institutions* (London: John Murray).

Malinowski, B. (1936), *Foundations of Faith and Morals* (London: Oxford University Press).

Mandeville, B. (1715/1924), *The Fable of the Bees,* ed. F. B. Kaye (Oxford: Clarendon Press).

Mayr, E. (1970), *Populations, Species, and Evolution* (Cambridge: Harvard University Press).

Mayr, E. (1982), *The Growth of Biological Thought* (Cambridge: Harvard University Press).

McCleary, G. F. (1953), *The Malthusian Population Theory* (London: Faber & Faber).

McNeill, William H. (1981), 'A Defence of World History', *Royal Society Lecture.*

Medawar, P. B. and J. S.(1983), *Aristotle to Zoos: A Philosophical Dictionary of Biology* (Cambridge: Harvard University Press).

Medick, Hans (1973), *Naturzustand und Naturgeschichte der bürgerlichen Gesellschaft; Die Ursprünge der bürgerlichen Sozialtheorie als Geschichtsphilosophie und Sozialwissenschaft bei Samuel Pufendorf, John Locke und Adam Smith* (Göttingen: Vandenhoeck & Ruprecht).

Menger, Carl (1871/1934/1981), *Principles of Economics* (New York and London: New York University Press). Reprinted in German by the London School of Economics in 1934, Vol. I: see below.

Menger, Carl (1883/1933/1985), *Problems of Economics and Sociology*, trans. Francis J. Nock, ed. Louis Schneider (Urbana: University of Illinois Press, 1963); republished as *Investigations into the Method of the Social Sciences with Special Reference to Economics*, with new introduction by Lawrence White (New York: New York University Press). Reprinted in German by the London School of Economics in 1933, Vol. II: see below.

Menger, Carl (1933–36), *The Collected Works of Carl Menger*, reprint in four volumes, in German (London: London School of Economics and Political Science (Series of Reprints of Scarce Tracts in Economic and Political Science, no. 17–20)).

Menger, Carl (1968–70), *Gesammelte Werke* (Tübingen: J. C. B. Mohr (Paul Siebeck) Verlag).

Mill, John Stuart (1848/1965), *Principles of Political Economy*, Vols. 2 and 3 of *Collected Works of John Stuart Mill*, ed. J. M. Robson (London: Routledge & Kegan Paul, Ltd.).

Miller, David (1976), *Social Justice* (Oxford: Oxford University Press).

Mises, Ludwig von (1949), *Human Action: A Treatise on Economics* (New Haven: Yale University Press).

Mises, Ludwig von (1957), *Theory and History* (New Haven: Yale University Press).

Mises, Ludwig von (1922/81): *Socialism* (Indianapolis: Liberty*Classics*, 1981).

Monod, Jacques (1970/77), *Chance and Necessity* (Glasgow: Collins/Fount paperback, 1977); first published as *Le hazard ou la necessité* (Paris: Editions du Seuil, 1970).

Monod, Jacques (1970), in A. Tiseliu and S. Nilsson, eds.: *The Place of Values in a World of Facts* (Stockholm: Nobel Symposium 14).

Montesquieu, Charles Louis de Secondat de (1748), *De l'Esprit des loix*, I (Geneva: Barrillot & Fils).

Moore, G. E. (1903), *Principia Ethica* (Cambridge: Cambridge University Press).

Myrdal, Gunnar (1960), *Beyond the Welfare State* (New Haven: Yale University Press).

Needham, Joseph (1943), *Time the Refreshing River* (London: Allen & Unwin).

Needham, Joseph (1954), *Science and Civilisation in China* (Cambridge: Cambridge University Press, 1954–85), in 6 volumes and numerous parts.

North, D. C. (1973) and R. P. Thomas, *The Rise of the Western World* (Cambridge: Cambridge University Press).

North, D. C. (1981), *Structure and Change in Economic History* (New York: W. W. Norton & Co.).

O'Brien, C. C. (1986), 'God and Man in Nicaragua', *The Atlantic 258*, August 1986.

Orwell, George (1937), *The Road to Wigan Pier* (London: V. Gollancz).

Patten, Simon N. (1899), *The Development of English Thought: A Study in the Economic Interpretation of History* (New York: The Macmillan Company; London: Macmillan and Co., Ltd.).

Pei, Mario (1978), *Weasel Words: The Art of Saying What You Don't Mean* (New York: Harper & Row).

Petty, William (1681/1899), 'The Growth, Increase and Multiplication of Mankind' (1681), in *The Economic Writings of Sir William Petty*, ed. C. H. Hull, vol. 2 (Cambridge: Cambridge University Press, 1899).

Petty, William (1927), *The Petty Papers: Some Unpublished Writings of Sir William Petty*, ed. Marquis of Lansdowne (London: Constable & Co.).

Piaget, Jean (1929), *The Child's Conception of the World* (London: K. Paul, Trench, Trubner & Co., Ltd.).

Pierson, N. G. (1902/1912), *Principles of Economics*, translated from the Dutch by A. A. Wotzel (London, New York: Macmillan and Co., Ltd.).

Piggott, Stuart (1965), *Ancient Europe from the beginning of Agriculture to Classical Antiquity* (Edinburgh: Edinburgh University Press).

Pirenne, J. (1934), *Histoire des institutions et du droit privé de l'ancienne Egypte* (Brussels: Edition de la Fondation Egyptologique Reine Elisabeth).

Polanyi, Karl (1945), *Origin of Our Time: The Great Transformation* (London: V. Gollancz, Ltd.).

Polanyi, Karl (1977), *The Livelihood of Man*, ed. H. W. Pearson (New York: Academic Press).

Popper, K. R. (1934/59), *The Logic of Scientific Discovery* (London: Hutchinson, 1959).

Popper, K. R. (1945/66), *The Open Society and Its Enemies* (London: Routledge and Kegan Paul, Ltd., sixth edition, 1966).

Popper, K. R. (1948/63), 'Towards a Rational Theory of Tradition', lecture given in 1948, published in *The Rationalist Annual*, 1949; reprinted in Popper (1963).

Popper, K. R. (1957), *The Poverty of Historicism* (London: Routledge & Kegan Paul, Ltd.).

Popper, K. R. (1963), *Conjectures and Refutations* (London: Routledge & Kegan Paul, Ltd.).

Popper, K. R. (1972), *Objective Knowledge: An Evolutionary Approach* (London: Oxford University Press).

Popper, K. R. (1974/76), 'Autobiography', in P. A. Schilpp, ed.: *The Philosophy of Karl Popper* (La Salle: Open Court, 1974), pp. 3–181, republished, revised, as *Unended Quest* (London: Fontana/Collins, 1976).

Popper, K. R. (1977/84) and J. C. Eccles, *The Self and Its Brain* (London: Routledge & Kegan Paul, Ltd., 1984).

Popper, Karl R. (1982a), *The Open Universe: An Argument for Indeterminism*, Vol. II of the *Postscript to the Logic of Scientific Discovery*, ed. W. W. Bartley, III (London: Hutchinson).

Popper, K. R. (1982b), *Quantum Theory and the Schism in Physics*, Vol. III of the *Postscript to the Logic of Scientific Discovery*, ed. W. W. Bartley, III (London: Hutchinson).

Popper, K. R. (1983), *Realism and the Aim of Science*, Vol. I of the *Postscript to the Logic of Scientific Discovery*, ed. W. W. Bartley, III (London: Hutchinson).

Pribram, K. (1983), *A History of Economic Reasoning* (Baltimore: Johns Hopkins University Press).

Prigogine, Ilya (1980), *From Being to Becoming: Time and Complexity in the Physical Sciences* (San Francisco: W. H. Freeman).

Quinton, A. (1977), 'Positivism', in *Harper/Fontana Dictionary of Modern Thought* (New York: Harper & Row).

Radnitzky, Gerard and W. W. Bartley, III, eds. (1987): *Evolutionary Epistemology, Rationality, and the Sociology of Knowledge* (La Salle: Open Court).

Rawls, John (1971), *A Theory of Justice* (Cambridge: Harvard University Press).

Renfrew, Colin (1972), *Emergence of Civilisation* (London: Methuen).

Renfrew, Colin (1973), *The Explanation of Culture Change: Models in Prehistory* (London: Duckworth).

Roberts, P. C. (1971), *Alienation in the Soviet Economy* (Albuquerque: University of New Mexico Press).

Rostovtzeff, M. (1930), 'The Decline of the Ancient World and its Economic Explanation', *Economic History Review*, II; *A History of the Ancient World* (Oxford: Clarendon Press); *L'empereur Tibère et le culte impérial* (Paris: F. Alcan), and *Gesellschaft und Wirtschaft im Römischen Kaiserreich* (Leipzig: Quelle & Meyer).

Rostovtzeff, M. (1933), Review of J. Hasebrock, *Griechische Wirtschafts-*

und Handelsgeschichte, in *Zeitschrift für die gesamte Staatswirtschaft 92*, pp. 333–39.

Rousseau, Jean–Jacques (1762), *Social Contract*.

Ruse, Michael (1982), *Darwinism Defended: A Guide to the Evolution Controversies* (Reading, Mass.: Addison-Wesley).

Russell, Bertrand (1931), *The Scientific Outlook* (New York: W. W. Norton & Company, Inc.).

Russell, Bertrand (1940), 'Freedom and Government' in R. N. Anshen, ed., *Freedom, Its Meaning* (New York: Harcourt, Brace & Co.).

Russell, Bertrand (1910/1966), *Philosophical Essays*, revised edition (London: Allen & Unwin).

Rutland, Peter (1985), *The Myth of the Plan: Lessons of Soviet Planning Experience* (London: Hutchinson).

Ryle, Gilbert (1945–46) 'Knowing How and Knowing That', *Proceedings of the Aristotelian Society 46*.

Ryle, Gilbert (1949), *The Concept of Mind* (London: Hutchinson's University Library).

Savigny, F. C. (1814/31), *Vom Beruf unserer Zeit für Gesetzgebung und Rechtswissenschaft* (Heidelberg: Mohr und Zimmer, 1814), trans. Abraham Hayward, as *Of the Vocation of Our Age for Legislation and Jurisprudence* (London: Littlewood & Co., 1831).

Savigny, F. C. (1840), *System des heutigen Römischen Rechts* (Berlin: Veit, 1840–49).

Schelsky, H. (1975), *Die Arbeit tun die Anderen* (Opladen: Westdeutscher Verlag).

Schiller, J. C. F. (1793), *Über die ästhetische Erziehung des Menschen*, in *Sämtliche Werke* (Stuttgart und Tübingen: J. G. Cotta, 1812–15), Vol. 8; republished as *Über die ästhetische Erziehung des Menschen in einer Reihe von Briefen*, Kurt Hoffmann, ed. (Bielefeld: Velhagen & Klasing, 1934).

Schoeck, Helmut (1973), 'Die Sprache des Trojanischen Pferd', in *Die Lust am schlechten Gewissen* (Freiburg: Herder).

Schoeck, Helmut (1966/69), *Envy* (London: Secker & Warburg).

Schrödinger, Erwin (1944), *What Is Life? The Physical Aspect of the Living Cell* (Cambridge, The University Press).

Schulze, H. (1913), *Deutsches Fremdwörterbuch*.

Schumacher, E. F. (1973), *Small Is Beautiful* (New York: Harper & Row).

Schumpeter, J. (1954), *History of Economic Analysis* (New York: Oxford University Press).

Scitovsky, Tibor (1976), *The Joyless Economy: an Inquiry into Human Satisfaction and Consumer Dissatisfaction* (New York: Oxford University Press).

Segerstedt, Torgny (1969), 'Wandel der Gesellschaft', in *Bild der Wissenschaft 6.*

Seton–Watson, H. (1983), *Times Literary Supplement*, 18 November, p. 1270.

Shafarevich, Igor Rostislavovich (1975/1980), *The Socialist Phenomenon* (New York: Harper & Row).

Simon, Julian L. (1977), *The Economics of Population Growth* (Princeton: Princeton University Press).

Simon, Julian L. (1978), ed., *Research in Population Economics* (Greenwich, Conn.: JAI Press).

Simon, Julian L. (1981a), 'Global Confusion, 1980: A Hard Look at the Global 2000 Report', in *The Public Interest 62.*

Simon, Julian L. (1981b), *The Ultimate Resource* (Princeton: Princeton University Press).

Simon, Julian L. and Hermann Kahn, eds. (1984), *The Resourceful Earth* (Oxford: Basil Blackwell).

Simpson, G. G. (1972), 'The Evolutionary Concept of Man', in B. G. Campbell, ed., *Sexual Selection and the Descent of Man, 1871–1971* (Chicago: Aldine Publishing Co.).

Skinner, B. F. (1955–56), 'Freedom and the Control of Man', *American Scholar 25*, pp. 47–65.

Smith, Adam (1759), *Theory of Moral Sentiments* (London: A. Millar).

Smith, Adam (1759/1911), *Theory of Moral Sentiments* (London: G. Bell and Sons).

Smith, Adam (1776/1976), *An Inquiry into the Nature and Causes of the Wealth of Nations* (Oxford: Oxford University Press, 1976).

Smith, Adam (1978), *Lectures on Jurisprudence*, ed. R. L. Meek, D. D. Raphael, P. G. Stein (Oxford: Clarendon Press).

Sombart, Werner (1902), *Der moderne Kapitalismus* (Leipzig: Duncker & Humblot).

Stein, Peter (1966), *Regulae Iuris* (Edinburgh: University Press).

Stewart, Dugald (1828/1854–60), *Works*, ed. W. Hamilton (Edinburgh: T. Constable).

Strabo, *The Geography of Strabo*, trans. Horace L. Jones (London: Heinemann, 1917).

Sullivan, James (1795), *The Altar of Baal thrown down; or, the French Nation defended against the pulpit slander of David Osgood* (Philadelphia: Aurora Printing Office).

Teilhard de Chardin, P. (1959), *The Phenomenon of Man*, (New York: Harper).

Thorpe, W. H. (1963), *Learning and Instinct in Animals* (London: Methuen).

Thorpe, W. H. (1966/76), *Science, Man, and Morals* (Ithaca: Cornell

171

University Press); republished (Westport, Conn: Greenwood Press, 1976).

Thorpe, W. H. (1969), *Der Mensch in der Evolution*, with an introduction by Konrad Lorenz (München: Nymphenburger Verlagshandlung). Translation of *Science, Man and Morals* (Ithaca: Cornell University Press, 1966).

Thorpe, W. H. (1978), *Purpose in a World of Chance* (Oxford: Oxford University Press).

Trotter, Wilfred (1916), *Instincts of the Herd in Peace and War* (London: T. F. Unwin, Ltd.).

Tylor, Edward B. (1871), *Primitive Culture* (London: J. Murray).

Ullmann–Margalit, Edna (1977), *The Emergence of Norms* (Oxford: Clarendon Press).

Ullmann–Margalit, Edna (1978), 'Invisible Hand Explanations', *Synthese 39*, 1978.

United Nations (1980), 'Concise Report of the World Population Situation in 1979: Conditions, Trends, Prospects and Policies', *United Nations Population Studies 72*.

Vico, G. (1854), *Opere*, 2nd ed., ed. G. Ferrari (Milan).

Vorzimmer, Peter J. (1977), *Charles Darwin: the Years of Controversy; The Origin of Species and Its Critics, 1859–1882* (Philadelphia: Temple University Press).

Wells, H. G. (1984), *Experience in Autobiography* (London: Faber & Faber).

Westermarck, E. A. (1906–08), *The Origin and Development of the Moral Ideas* (London: MacMillan and Co.).

Wieland, C. M. (1800), *Aristipp und einige seiner Zeitgenossen* (Leipzig: B. G. J. Göschen).

Wiese, Leopold von (1917), *Der Liberalismus in Vergangenheit und Zukunft* (Berlin: S. Fischer).

Williams, George C., ed. (1966), *Adaptation and Natural Selection* (Princeton: Princeton University Press).

Williams, George C. (1971), *Group Selection* (Chicago: Aldine–Atherton).

Williams, George C. (1975), *Sex and Evolution* (Princeton: Princeton University Press).

Williams, Raymond (1976), *Key Words: A Vocabulary of Culture and Society* (London: Fontana).

Wynne–Edwards, V. C. (1962), *Animal Dispersion in Relation to Social Behaviour* (Edinburgh: Oliver & Boyd).

NAME INDEX

Acton, Lord, 52
Alchian, Armen, 36, 118, 159
Alland, A. Jr., 16, 159
Alvarez, Louis W., 148, 159
Aquinas, (Saint) Thomas, 47–8, 146
Aristotle, 11, 32, 45–8, 52, 90, 104,
  109–10, 146

Babbage, Charles, 87, 159
Baechler, Jean, 33, 45, 159
Bailey, Samuel, 15, 159
Barker, Ernest, 159
Barrett, Paul H., 24
Barry, Brian, 50, 54, 159
Bartley, W.W. III, 10, 61, 68, 91, 159
Bateson, William, 147, 159
Bauer, Lord (Peter Bauer), 125, 160
Baumgardt, D., 160
Becker, G.S., 36
Bell, Daniel, 160
Bentham, Jeremy, 52, 63, 65, 107, 146,
  160
Bernal, J.D., 60
Bernstam, Mikhail, 158
Bloch, Ernst, 107, 160
Blum, H.F., 151, 160
Blundell, John, xii
Böhm-Bawerk, Eugen von, 98, 150
Bonner, John Tyler, 17, 25, 160
Bopp, Franz, 147, 160
Born, Max, 60–1, 160
Boserup, Esther, 125, 160
Boswell, James, 32
Braudel, Ferdinand, 100, 103, 108, 111,
  160
Brien, Timothy, 158
Bullock, Allan, 160
Burke, Edmund, 29, 35, 53, 160
Butler, Samuel, 38, 161

Camara, (Archbishop) Hélden, 104
Campbell, B.G., 16, 161
Campbell, Donald T., 8, 18, 161

Campbell, W. Glenn, xii
Carlyle, Thomas, 91, 147, 161
Carr–Saunders, A.M., 16, 156, 161
Cato the Elder, 103
Chagnon, Napoleon A., 16, 161
Chapman, J.W., 113, 161
Cheung, Steven Ng Sheong, 36
Childe, V. Gordon, 22, 39, 156, 161
Chisholm, G.B., 58, 67
Cicero, Marcus Tullius, 11, 32, 103
Clark, Grahame, 161
Clark, R.W., 59, 161
Clifford, W.K., 108
Coase, R.H., 36, 161
Cohen, J.E., 128, 161
Cohen, Morris R., 56, 59, 110, 161
Cohn, Norman, 162
Columbus, Christopher, 18
Comte, August, 26, 52, 68, 108, 162
Confucius, 106, 109, 162
Cubitt, Charlotte, 5, 158
Curran, Charles, 118, 162

Dairaines, Serge, 33, 162
Darwin, Charles, 23–4, 26, 70, 107–8,
  146–7
Demandt, Alexander, 110, 162
Demsetz, Harold, 36
Descartes, René, 48, 52
Durham, William, 162

Eccles, Sir John, 16, 162
Eddington, Sir Arthur, 60
Edmonds, J.M., 162
Einaudi, Luigi, 44, 162
Einstein, Albert, 58–60, 62, 67, 104, 162
Emmett, Dorothy M., 146, 162
Erhard, Ludwig, 117
Evans-Pritchard, E.E., 108, 162
Everett, C.W., 146, 162

Farb, Peter, 16, 162
Ferguson, Adam, 3, 35, 145–6, 162

173

SUBJECT INDEX

alienation, sources of, 64, Appendix D
altruism, as source of unhappiness, 64;
  can hinder formation of extended
  order, 81; in small groups, 18–19
animism, abandoned in transcendent
  self-ordering process, 73; in
  connotation of words, 107; in
  interpretation of complex structures,
  82; persistence in studies of human
  affairs, 108; in religion, 56
anthropomorphism, see *animism*
'artificial' (as opposed to 'natural'),
  confusion caused by Hume's use of,
  145; as product of design, 143;
  Appendix A
Austrian school of economics, 97–8; see
  also *marginal utility*

beneficial ends, foreknowledge of, as
  absurd requirement for action in
  extended order, 80–1
benevolent despotism, 117
Benthamite tradition, 52, 146
biological evolution, differences from
  cultural evolution, 25; does not
  entirely predate cultural evolution,
  22; how change occurs in, 15; not
  subject to inevitable laws, 26; and
  studies of cultural development, 24
Bloomsbury Group, 57
Boswell's *Life* (Dr. Samuel Johnson), 32
calculus of lives, 132
capacity for learning, in humans, 18, 21,
  79
capital, Marx's work on, 150; to support
  population, 124–5
capitalism, 6; and belief that owners
  manipulate system, 78, 82; and
  civilisation, 9; created proletariat,
  124; creates employment, 123;
  expansion of, 33; fails to satisfy tenets
  of constructivist rationalism, 66; and
  freedom, 62–3; resistance to its

practices, 9; use of dispersed
  knowledge in, 9; use of term, 111
catallactics, 62, 98, 112
central authority, rule by, 6; compared
  to operation of decentralized market,
  86–7; inability to produce fullest use
  of information, 77, 86–7; inability to
  produce 'social justice' and economic
  improvement, 85; and several
  property, 50
civil liberties, 29
civilisation, benefits and costs, xi; and
  cultural evolution, 17; and extended
  order, 6; foundations in antiquity, 29;
  historical conflicts, 18; limited role of
  strong government in advance of,
  32–3; not made by conscious design,
  22; resulted from unwanted gradual
  changes in morality, 20; restrains
  instinctual behavior, 12; and several
  property, 29, 34
Civilisation and its Discontents (Sigmund
  Freud), xi, 18
collective product, magnitude of, 7
collective utility, not discoverable, 98
collectivism, and primitive man, 12; and
  wider trade relations, 42
commerce, in ancient world, 29; Spartan
  attitude toward, 32; in spread of
  civilisation, 34
competition, of currencies, not allowed
  by government monopoly, 103; in
  evolution, 26; and observance of rules,
  19; as procedure of discovery in
  adapting to unknown circumstances,
  19; required to prevent abuse of
  property, 35
conservatism, not Hayek's position
  except in limited moral issues, 53
constructivist rationalism, 22; in
  attempt to control development, 22;
  biases archaeology and sociology,
  50–1; embodies false theory of reason,